Building a Just Society

**To Maurice Bishop,
for inspiring this book**

Building a Just Society

A Different Viewpoint

Patrick Bascio

Maryknoll, New York 10545

The Catholic Foreign Mission Society of America (Maryknoll) recruits and trains people for overseas missionary service. Through Orbis Books Maryknoll aims to foster the international dialogue that is essential to mission. The books published, however, reflect the opinions of their authors and are not meant to represent the official position of the society.

Copyright © 1981 Orbis Books, Maryknoll, NY 10545
All rights reserved
Manufactured in the United States of America

Library of Congress Cataloging in Publication Data

Bascio, Patrick.
  Building a Just Society

  1. Communism and Christianity. 2. Communism and Christianity—Catholic Church. I. Title.
HX536.B298   261.2'1   80-27238
ISBN 0-88344-205-1 (pbk.)

CONTENTS

Preface   vii
1. A Different Viewpoint   1
2. Patricia Sullivan, Communist and Friend   13
3. Thanksgiving at Dorothy Day's   29
4. A Christian Response to Marxism?   40
5. Marxism, Communism, and communism: The Difference   47
6. Communism, the Christian Ideal   59
7. The Diplomat   73
8. A Tribute to Jamal Baroody   93
9. The Decline of a Marxist   102
10. May Marx Rest in Peace   116
11. Karl Marx and Religion   124
12. Eurocommunism   134
13. The Economic Consequences of Marxist Ideology for the West   141

Preface

The spirit of crisis in the Church to which Pope Paul VI often referred is sometimes rather simplistically reduced to the crises of clerics searching for identity. This is understandable since the most visible and dramatic event which can happen at the parochial level (where the people are) is the departure of a priest from the ministry. These departures, however, are symptoms and not the problem itself, although no one would deny that they exacerbate, dramatize, and further confuse whatever it is that lies beneath the surface.

The real problem, the one that produces the visible symptoms of defections and functional disabilities, is the absence of a strong, articulate, and mature incarnation of the Church in the modern world. But this alienation is not peculiar to the Church alone. Western society is in crisis. We are witnesses to the crisis of Western civilization. Jacques Maritain pointed out years ago that the sacred age has already died, but our institutions have operated as though they were still motivated by codes of ethics and modes of thought that have long since disappeared from the marketplace. It was inevitable that this pretense would get thinner and thinner, as the society began to function more and more in tune with reality.

Those of us who function in the Church and receive our inspiration, strength, and sustenance from the Church have been too prone to lay the blame for the increasing alienation of human beings from their society on the Church. This is unfair, since the institutional Church is but a reflection of the general state of humankind at any given time in history. The fact is that we have come to the end of the long era of Western Christendom, not of Christianity. It is only an accident of history that the Church's development has been co-extensive with the rise and fall of the West. For this reason, the Church has often been mistakenly identified with a decaying and increasingly ineffectual culture. The situation is not helped, of course, by the fact that many in the Church have insisted on identifying Christianity with their own culture, adding to the confusion and disorientation surrounding the question of the Church in the modern world. What is happening is not the end of religion, but rather the beginning of a new and emerging world, and the Church will no doubt become a factor in the transformation of that world. This will not become evident until the decay of the West runs its course, and the economic and structural transformations which are so evidently destined to occur begin to emerge.

The Latin American bishops, at the Medellín Conference in 1968, made many prophetic statements, among which was the following:

> We are at the beginning of a new historic epoch in our continent. It is filled with the hope of total emancipation—liberation from all servitude—personal maturity, and collective integration. We foresee the painful gestation of a new civilization [Medellín Documents, Message to the Peoples of Latin America].

Historically, the Church has become so intimately entwined with Western culture that it is not a bit surprising

Preface

that, institutionally, it will also go through a period of decay. At the close of the first session of Vatican II, Cardinal Suenens pointed out that the cultural forms into which the Christian message has been poured must always be subject to a re-examination in order to protect the integrity of that message. And if the cultural form be found wanting, then with great delicacy but also with firmness, the Church must adopt other cultural forms more in conformity with its message. Pope John XXIII, in his opening speech to the Council Fathers, agreed:

> It is one thing to speak of the substance of ancient doctrine contained in the deposit of faith and another the formulation in which it is vested. We must give great importance to this form and work patiently, if necessary, at its elaboration.

We need not fear for religion or for the Church; both are alive and well. They are waiting in the wings for the final curtain to fall on Western Graeco-Roman civilization as we have known it. We have entered the age of socialization and humanization in which humankind has become the center and principal mover of the world and human history. It has been a long time coming to fulfillment but its impetus was given at the beginning:

> So God created man in his own image; in the image of God he created him; male and female he created them. God blessed them and said to them, "Be fruitful and increase, fill the earth and subdue it, rule over the fish in the sea, the birds of heaven, and every living thing that moves upon the earth" [Gen. 1:27–28.]

The renewed cultural incarnation of the Church in the

world awaits the further delineation of this new cultural form because only then will the Church know the horizontal and vertical dimensions of its new incarnation. Those who complain that Vatican II has never been properly implemented fail to understand that there is no way in which the progressive and sacred changes proposed by the bishops at the Council can be incarnated in the presently structured Western society. They could probably more easily be assimilated into the newly emerging socialist nations. Can you imagine a company executive, though he may be a church-going Christian, abandoning the one thing that motivates his life, the maximization of profits? Vatican II is a spirit going around looking for a body to inhabit, and when that body comes along the Church will become a vital and significant factor in the next stage of the development of humankind. We criticize the Church for having been a part of the establishment, and this is a very myopic view. The establishment is the reflection of ourselves. It is our flesh and blood, it is our humanity reaching out to the world. It is not the establishment that is the problem; it is the already-decayed cultural form that supports it.

It should not shock us to hear that Western civilization is dying. After all, it has been around since the Graeco-Roman days, so it certainly cannot complain of having had too short a life-span. It created the scientific and technological ages. It brought the development of art, music, and poetry to every niche and corner of Europe and the Americas. It colonized the non-Western world, passing on to it the fruits of its enlightenment. Its scrapbook is full of a million pictures. It can now die, contented in the knowledge that it has led a long and glorious life and that perhaps it can be forgiven the waywardness it displayed in its latter days of senility. Money and its pursuit became the cancer that killed it, but this was only fitting since it was money that made it grow and that sustained its long and glorious career. Lewis H. Lapham, an editor of *Harper's* magazine, in an article entitled "The Capitalist Paradox," says it all:

They present me with evidence of graft in Washington or St. Louis, . . . of payoffs, bribes, and stock-market swindles. . . . I cannot help but be surprised by the innocence of my informants. . . . I take for granted Jefferson's dictum that money, not morality, constitutes the principle of commercial nations.

The continuous history of creating great wealth by simultaneously creating great poverty and social distress has finally caught up with us. Aristotle's remark that poverty is the parent of revolution and violence is even more true today than when he said it 2,500 years ago. And is it not ironic that the creators of great wealth have corrupted Western civilization, and that those whom they have impoverished are now creating the new age? The meek are going to inherit the earth.

It is too early to tell what the new age is going to be like, but a shift in economic structures appears to be the first fruit. For some reason known only to the Creator, the predispositions needed to welcome the new age have been formed and articulated outside the Church, and often in opposition to it. Karl Marx has let loose on the world a terrestrial messianism which preaches the end of our alienation from ourselves. The task of the Church will be to envelop this new secularism with the protective shield of grace and divine inspiration so as to prevent a catastrophe of exaggerated egoism and self-aggrandizement. This will be the task of the Church and we must face it with faith, hope, and ingenuity. It is of no use to hide behind the old forms, hoping that the terrestrial messianism will fade away. Let the Church look to "the signs of the times" in a world of revolutionary ferment and direction.

In the early stages of addressing ourselves to the contents of the secular age, we are bound to run into many difficulties and make many mistakes. In Trinidad, in various forums, I spoke about economic and cultural alternatives, and a local newspaper, *The Bomb,* which is said to reflect government policies, accused me of being a Communist. The editor, Patrick Chookolingo, knew better than that and relented to the extent of allowing me a reply, which he was kind enough to print. My reply to *The Bomb* read in part:

> Dear Mr. Chookolingo:
> Permit me to comment on your article: "Communist or Catholic?"
> It is quite understandable that a priest who discusses the value of private property, alienation, or the theory of surplus value can easily be misunderstood. Add to this the fact that he may be on friendly terms with men who for some reason or other have gained a reputation for being radical, and you have all the ingredients for such an article as appeared in *The Bomb.* I appreciate this and do not resent it.
> However, may I assure you personally that I have never been nor shall I ever be an advocate of atheistic and imperialistic Communism. My interest in exploring new approaches to the perennial problems of poverty has led me to read and discuss far and wide, but always within the context of the simple gospel message of Jesus.
> Marx's analysis of alienation and surplus value can be added, without fear, to the patrimony of human

Preface

wisdom, just as Julius Nyerere's "Ujamaa" has made a significant contribution to the economic and cultural development of Tanzania. I need only add that Dom Helder Camara's stature throughout the academic world is a further indication that the gospel message has within it the seeds of the resolution of human misery.

I hope that this brief letter allays your quite reasonable fears and puts my work into its proper perspective.

God bless you and keep you always.

Father Patrick

I hope that this letter will also allay some of the fears that may be generated by reading the following pages.

This preface would not be complete without a reference to Norma Blaize, the daughter of former Grenada Prime Minister Herbert Blaize.

While disenchanted with conventional politics, she nevertheless has been, for me, a wonderful source of wisdom and knowledge, not only about West Indian politics and politicians, but also about the delicate mystery of the relationships obtaining between peoples of different cultural worldviews.

1
A Different Viewpoint

We want to fix a steady gaze on those who still lack the opportune help to achieve a way of life worthy of human beings [Message to Humanity, *Vatican II*].

At the Second Vatican Council, the bishops reaffirmed, though in less strident tones than previously, that the principal task of the Church is to teach and to sanctify. The Church claims to have the deposit of the truth handed down to us by the Father, through his Son, Jesus Christ. No other earthly power claims such wide-sweeping authority or righteousness. In fact no other earthly power or organization would even dare to assume so great a burden, so exalted a position. A rather frequently heard saying is "All religions pray to the same God, so we are all headed in the same direction." This is not true for the Church. There are two principal beliefs held by Christians throughout the world. "We believe in one God, the Father Almighty . . . and . . . in one Lord Jesus Christ." The second belief is "We believe in one, holy, catholic, and apostolic Church." Christians believe that one Church only is the Church of Jesus Christ; one Church alone teaches the undiluted doctrine of Jesus Christ, sent by God himself, to educate, sanctify, and save the entire world.

Nothing in the writings of Mao Zedong's "little Red Book" can match this magnificent and sweeping claim to divine power and guidance. Christians are either correct or they are the greatest egotists the world has ever seen. And what makes this position either magnificently correct or tragically wrong is that the position is held, not from logic nor from historical proof, but from faith. Not that either logic or historical evidence is lacking. But we prefer to "believe" in one God rather than try to prove that God exists. We "believe" in one, holy, catholic, and apostolic Church. We don't really demand, unconditionally, that someone provide historical evidence. And this makes good sense. We are dealing here, not with the material world, where empirical evidence can give at least relative satisfaction, but with a divinity of which we know absolutely nothing for sure. And so we "believe" in one God, in Jesus Christ, his Son, and in one, holy, catholic Church. We believe that Christ is the light of all nations and that this light, or torch, is being borne through the ages by the Church. The Church is, in some mysterious way, Christ among us.

Having made this extraordinary claim, it behooves the Church to live up to its image, one that it has painted of itself. This self-portrait has been painted with broad and bold strokes. The Church claims to have the deposit of truth, to be the Church of Christ, the Teacher of humankind. It cannot now, after such public proclamation, retreat to a narcissistic position of personal salvation. It dare not say, now, that it has nothing to do with the ordinary affairs of humankind. It cannot, without great loss of credibility, refuse to comment on political and economic systems. Either it is the light of the world, or it is not. It cannot have it both ways.

After stating that Christ brought to us the kingdom of God on earth, the Church cannot then pretend that he

A Different Viewpoint

brought us the kingdom of heaven, in heaven. It cannot attempt to mold the clay that human beings are made of without dirtying its fingers. It is trapped, by its own self-definition, into proclaiming the morality of all earthly things. After having proclaimed itself the Body of Christ, the light of all the nations, the door that leads to the Father, the edifice of God, the Holy City, and the New Jerusalem, it is unbecoming to hide behind a false modesty when asked to declare the truth and to show the way in humankind's pilgrimage on earth. A pilgrim Church without pilgrims and a pilgrimage is in a rather awkward condition.

In a teeming world of youthful revolution, black consciousness, women's rights, gay rights, and the dislocation of traditional political and economic systems, the Church cannot close the doors and windows of its house and refuse to communicate with the world. It should be and no doubt will one day be a paradigm of a transition between old and new potentialities. It must achieve, as in the Middle Ages, that unity of theory and practice which is the condition for its usefulness to the world. Not those who cry Abba are in harmony with the Father, but those who do the will of the Father. As teacher, its chief pedagogical tool must be the praxis of the community of nations, not the outmoded, incomplete, even unjust principles of another age and lifestyle. The Church must so declare itself that it will be possible to unite theory and praxis in the church community without having the church burned down. What relevance does the agony of the Cross have to humankind if the possibility of agony today for justice' sake is considered unacceptable by Christians?

Given the natural conservatism of people and the fact that, after all, the hierarchy of the Church is composed of mortals, it is not surprising that such a huge and cumbersome entity as the institutional Church should be slow to change. It is faced with the embarrassing fact that a long-time friend, one in whom it has had confidence for hundreds of years, is becoming decadent and corrupt. The capitalist system of economics (an entire culture of values and mores) was the savior of those who lived in abject poverty during the time of the economic system of feudalism. It was capitalism that built international trade, the large cities of which the West has been so proud until recent times, when it has been difficult even to collect the garbage, and the industrial giants which have provided jobs and affluence to an ever-growing number of the world's citizens.

Capitalism might have been historically necessary; in that sense it has played its role in history. But now it is increasingly being jettisoned as outmoded, unjust, unstable, and the root cause of a cancerous kind of corruption in society. Being a conservative institution it is not surprising that the Church has been slow to react to what is happening all around it. This is the nature of institutions and the Church is no more guilty of dragging its feet than any other public institution, perhaps even much less so. The time has indeed come for the Church to examine the moral effects of this corroding capitalist economic system and to bring forth innovative and gospel-centered answers to the problems of our time. It has done so in the past and there is no reason to think that it will not again do so in the future.

The last time that the institutional Catholic Church seriously examined itself and its policies was at the time of the Counter-Reformation. Being basically conservative, it waited until enormous damage had been done and countless millions of souls had abandoned the hope of spiritual salvation within its confines. The rise in influence of Luther, Calvin, Zwingli, and the Anglican Church in England, among other defections, finally caused the hierarchy to call a Council, at Trent, on December 3, 1545. This Council was to last eighteen years and it did in fact attack, in a forthright and courageous manner, the main problems of the time and, further, laid the foundations for their solutions. Even before the Council was called, Pope Paul II had appointed a commission to study Church reform. This commission produced a surprisingly honest document cataloging the corruption and abuses rife in the Church called "The Council of Cardinals on Reforming the Church." So impressed was Martin Luther with the candidness of this report that he had it translated into German and distributed to his followers.

The Counter-Reformation had begun. The Church marshalled its considerable spiritual and intellectual potential and, in time, began to shine as the jewel that it cannot help being. But not only a spiritual reformation was afoot in those days. Decisions were being made in the field of economics which were to erode the economic system of feudalism and create the conditions under which capitalism was born and developed. The growth of the strength of the Counter-Reformation Church, coinciding as it did with new cultural and economic concepts, created a cultural atmosphere where both grew together in harmony and mutual admiration. The good produced by the Counter-Reformation and the widening economic visions of the scholars and churchmen of that time combined to make for a powerful thrust forward in the development of society. It was the origin of the partnership that was to develop between the Church and the economic system of capitalism. It was a new partnership for the Church, for up until that time, since Charlemagne, the partnership was between the Church and the state. That partnership lasted for more than a thousand years. Eventually, because of changing relationships and different economic circumstances, it died out.

The Church is now beset with a new reformation, a reformation far more subtle and complicated than the one of the Middle Ages. The reformation of the Middle Ages had to do with the corruption of a church; the reformation of today has to do with the corruption of society. The reformation of the Middle Ages had to do with the question of self-purification on the part of the Church. The current reformation has to do with the danger of involvement on the part of the Church. Will the Church be soiled by reaching out once again, as in the days of Charlemagne, and become involved in matters temporal? This is a legitimate fear, but perhaps the historical imperatives demand that this fear be overcome.

However the peoples of recent times have perceived the Church, it has become increasingly evident that a majority of the world's peoples now perceive it as having a vital role in the development of the new person. However much the Church, engrossed in personal salvation, may wish to run away from this perception, the world holds it accountable for the fulfillment of its mission of teaching and sanctifying. Jesus (and the Church) came not for the saved but for those who are lost. It is inescapable; uncomfortable, but inescapable.

The new reformation is the ever-increasing adoption by the world of a new economic and political lifestyle. The genesis of the new perception is attributable to the writings of Karl Marx. He has influenced and continues to influence hundreds of millions. Concerned as it rightly was with what it perceived as the atheistic content of Marx's writings and influence, the Church, unfortunately, focused on this one issue to the exclusion of everything else. While the Church has remained preoccupied with expressions of atheism, the Third World, ignoring this issue, has gone on to adjust its economic and political

A Different Viewpoint 7

lifestyle to the general thrust of the Marxist ideology. It is rather pitiful to observe, as I have at close quarters, a Church preoccupied (paranoiac) about the theological content of Marx's writings while a whole nation around it arises and adopts Marx's economic theory, completely unconcerned about his theology.

If the new reformers were to look at the doctrine of the Church they might at first assume that they had an ally in the global effort to eradicate the economic source of so many of the world's evils. Tragically, not only does the Church decline to offer help, but in fact vigorously defends the system to which it has been wedded for all these many years. But there are signs that the Counter-Reformation has begun. Christians in almost every nation are patiently trying to influence the institutional Church to take a good look at itself, where it is and what it stands for. They continually and patiently point out to the institutional Church that the question is not one of atheism (a subject which I can tell you, from my own personal experience, bores revolutionaries), but of a society ripe for change. The fact that Karl Marx was the first important figure to analyze and explain the decay of a culture is not what is important (except to the historian); what is important is an awareness that a culture is dying and that this has moral, economic, political, esthetic, and social consequences for humankind.

Gradual enlightenment and a deepening of the social conscience among the clergy and laity will inevitably lead to a reconsideration of the validity of the Church's posture vis-à-vis a changing world. Perhaps the first sign of this awareness comes in the writings of the liberation theologians and the political theologians like J. B. Metz. They are certainly moving in the direction of the unity of theory and practice. The growing awareness by these theologians of the enormous gap between theory and practice in a world where liberation is evolving in the streets of the Third World (now being captured almost daily by television) is itself a great value.

The hierarchy in many nations is becoming increasingly aware that those who advocate a redistribution of the enormous wealth of the West are not causing class struggle; they are eliminating it. The elimination of the class struggle should have no more powerful an ally than the Church; for the Church preaches consistently the complete equality of all as sons and daughters of the same Father. This growing awareness on the part of the clergy is illustrated in an issue of *Maryknoll* magazine. Ronald S. Michels, M.M., comments on the political situation in El Salvador:

> Something that struck me during the persecution is that the people who killed the priests and catechists, who wrote the laws and gave the orders, are all Catholics, which is a strange twist of history. Usually, the Church has been condemned by pagans or Communists. Here, the Church has been persecuted by Catholics.

How often words like these are being uttered all over the world!

People like Sister Gertrude give us hope for the future. Sister was headmistress of the finest convent school on the island-nation of Grenada, in the West Indies. This island is a good example of what can happen in a society where intellectual and spiritual stagnation is strong but where events move an entire society to the praxis of revolutionary liberation. Sister Gertrude was an unyielding critic of my work of attempting to develop a revolutionary consciousness on that beautiful Caribbean island. But Sister did have a sense of fairness and an intuition that not all was well with the spiritual life of the island, in spite of being heavily influenced by the Catholic Church. I received a phone call from Sister one day, asking if I cared to teach religion to the senior classes "to balance off the ideas we nuns are imparting to our students. You, Father, can expose them to a different viewpoint." I admired her courage, for I know that it caused her difficulties within her own community.

Some of the nuns feared that my presence in the convent classroom was a provocation to the government of the then Prime Minister, Eric Gairy, a man who did not tolerate dissent and who already had referred to me at a Cabinet meeting as "the Communist priest, who is plaguing our peace-loving island." Many of the parents of the girls were uneasy and while I got along well with them personally, I could detect the tensions. Sister Gertrude was on the spot, and each time I met her at the school I was prepared to be asked to discontinue my class there. Instead, Sister moved in the opposite direction by inviting me to celebrate Mass once a week at the convent. "This will give you an opportunity to present your view of the Church's role in the world," she said. "But please, Father, be gentle. There are some very sensitive ladies here."

The two years I spent in close contact with the convent nuns was good for all concerned. For my part, in spite of my active involvement in the political life of the nation, I was able to stay close to the traditional piety and otherworldliness of the institutional Church, the source of our spiritual vitality, the vine from which we dare not be isolated branches. On their part, the nuns and young students began to view the socio-political situation in Grenada within the context of the ancient destructiveness of slavery and colonialism.

Their continued exposure to a different viewpoint led to their political activism. About a year after I left the island, the convent was accused by Prime Minister Gairy in the Parliament of being a hotbed of revolutionary thinking and plotting. The convent was searched on more than one occasion for arms, and the sisters were harassed. The recent Grenadian Ambassador to Washington and the United Nations, Kenrick Radix, took refuge behind those convent walls as government agents tried to track him down. On one very hot and humid afternoon, a senior girl at the convent led a large demonstration of students to the Prime Minister's office. As she was shouting her revolutionary intentions, we observed Gairy running out of his office as surreptitiously as he could to a public bathroom, where he had intended to hide. Apparently he feared that the students were going to rush into his office. The crowd of students moved to the locked men's room, and the comments that were shouted out to the trapped Prime Minister, while not fit to print, would be hilarious on a TV show.

The nuns and students in time came to understand that their vocation as Christians demanded that they risk everything in order to effectively reach out and bring peace and justice on earth. They had, symbolically, torn down the high convent walls and allowed themselves to touch the people and to be touched by them. The nuns continued to refuse to advocate Marxist ideology but they supported, with great personal danger, the young Marxists. This is typical of enlightened Christians wherever tyranny and oppression constitute the fabric of society. Religious men and women in many parts of the Third World are opposing Marxism in theory and supporting

A Different Viewpoint 11

Marxists in practice. Political conscientization has not kept up with the love and compassion they feel for their people, but there is no doubt that they are gradually learning, at first hand, the moral implications of political and economic systems. This is the thrust of history:

> Humanity has just entered what is probably the greatest transformation it has ever known; something is happening in the structure of human consciousness. It is another species of life that is just beginning [Teilhard de Chardin].

Karl Marx needs no defender. His work speaks for itself. He has inspired the restructuring of many societies. It seems that almost every few months another nation has transformed itself using the writings of Karl Marx as its guide. It is far more damaging to the spirituality of the Christian community to hate Marxists than to adopt Marxist ideology. Marxism has become synonymous with what we Christians do not like and, by a dangerous transmutation, what we don't like is thereby Marxism. Before our Christian world becomes irrelevant and jingoistic, we must somehow be shaken out of this narcissistic trance. The world needs the Church; it needs the bread that has come down from heaven. And the world includes all, Marxists and non-Marxists alike. Leopold Sedar Senghor, President of Senegal and black Africa's most renowned poet, reflects the thinking of many revolutionaries: "We realized that if Marxism could help cure our underdevelopment, it couldn't satisfy our spiritual hunger.

I look forward to the day when the Church, realizing that the search for social justice and a better economic system is not inimical to religion, will cease its distrust of social reformers.

The chapters that follow speak of my conviction that we are mutilating the Body of Christ by continuing our hate campaign against the Marxist community. I will speak of my love for every Marxist, my understanding of what Marxists are about, and my fervent prayer that their needs, their spiritual needs, will someday be ministered unto by a Church which has rediscovered its mission. I hope that I will live to see the day.

2
Patricia Sullivan, Communist and Friend

In his book *True Humanism*, Jacques Maritain has a chapter about the Communists. He says of them that by their dedication and self-sacrifice they were much closer to the God they denied than they or others suspected. Maritain, while not conferring sanctity on any of them, does not exclude Communists from the kingdom of heaven. This must have been a very daring statement on his part since the book goes back many years now. Some of what he had to say would be "fightin' words" even today in our average parish, a fact that illustrates how slowly the insights and compassion of our outstanding prophets seep into our consciousness.

When you think about it, all Maritain was saying was that people who dedicate themselves to the betterment of others and do so with sincerity and a spirit of self-sacrifice must be in good standing with God even if they do not believe in God. Surely, such disbelief could be no more than cerebral in a person whose heart burns with divine justice and charity. Of course, a theologian might counter: "But these acts were posited in a merely natural manner, not infused with sanctifying grace, so they have no merit toward eternal salvation."

Now, I am not going to take on the theologians, but my feeling is that such arguments are hollow and specious and not worthy of the Christian mentality. Not that our theologians are un-Christian, but there is a certain mind-construct that develops from the academic training that characterized our study of theology years ago. I think about this every time the anniversary of Patricia Sullivan's death rolls round. I don't think anyone has ever written about her, but to me she is a very important person and I would like a lot of people to know about her.

I first learned of Patricia Sullivan when, as a young Air Force Cadet at the University of Vermont in 1944, I dated her sister, Claire. I was seventeen then, and flying was my whole world. I lived with fellow cadets in Converse Hall on the university campus in Burlington. Claire was working in the cafeteria and we fell in love on the mess line. I finally got myself invited to Claire's home, out near what was then the only Howard Johnson's in Burlington. Claire's mother, Mom Sullivan, was one of the most delicate and poetic of women. She introduced me to Robert Frost, Walt Whitman, and John Donne. Her delicate femininity, perpetually encased in attractive attire of flowered patterns, lacy frills, and exquisite perfumes, pleased many a visitor. I spent as much, if not more, time with her as I did with Claire. She seemed to know everything about the whole world, and I would chat with her for hours. It was during one of these chats that she told me about her daughter Patricia. At first, she spoke about her almost in the abstract, usually in reference to her son, John, who was an officer in the diplomatic service. He was a man very much devoted to his country, and the bond between him and his mother was very strong. Patricia was a member of the Communist Party in New York, and had embarrassed her brother by sending him a subscription to the *Daily Worker*.

On one of my visits from Massachusetts I was told by Mom Sullivan of her latest and most tragic encounter with her daughter. She had recently returned from New York where she had visited Patricia, who was lying seriously ill in the hospital. Mrs. Sullivan began to say some of her prayers, and Patricia reached out for a bottle of ink sitting on her bed stand, flinging it at her mother. She screamed at her, told her to get out and never to visit her again. Her mother was devastated and bewildered. This incident certainly reinforced the image I had of the average Communist, and I felt a great resentment against the girl who could hurt such a loving and delicate woman. But there was soon to be a loving reunion between mother and daughter. They mutually agreed never to bring up the subject of religion again. Patricia said this would establish peace between them, and she reassured her mother that she loved her very much.

I entered the seminary to study for the priesthood in 1950 and saw little of the Sullivans over the next few years although I did correspond with Mom Sullivan and she kept me informed of her relationship with her Communist daughter. I would often receive a stipend for a Mass to be said for her daughter's return to the Catholic faith, and I spent many hours in the seminary chapel praying for this intention.

Ordination came in 1955, and in 1956 I was sent from the seminary in Norwalk, Connecticut, to St. Mark's Church in Harlem, at 138th Street and Lenox Avenue. This was a temporary assignment until autumn when I was to leave for Tanganyka (now Tanzania) in East Africa. I was very excited about being in Harlem, an experience I had waited for since entering the seminary. The lifestyle, attitudes, and aspirations of the black people had completely captivated me, and I often fancied myself having been born black and having that ability for self-expression that I admired so much in black people. I began to explore Harlem and got to know most of the street people by name. It took a lot of walking along hot New York City streets but I loved every minute of it.

One of my walking safaris brought me past Sydenham Hospital, where Patricia Sullivan worked. Patricia Sullivan, the Communist daughter of my lovely Victorian, Irish Catholic lady. On impulse, I bounded up the steps and into the hospital. At the main desk I asked if I could see Miss Sullivan. We had never met, though she knew of me from Mom Sullivan and had even told her mother many times that she would like to meet me. But that was before I was ordained a priest. How she would feel about getting to know me now, especially in view of her complete and even bitter abandonment of Catholicism, was another question. And I guess I was not mentally prepared to meet a young woman who had turned her back on a middle-class, suburban, Catholic atmosphere, to immerse herself in the foreign ideology of communism, which stood in antagonistic contrast to everything that made up my socio-cultural background. I felt threatened, but something kept me moving up to the area where I was told I would find her office.

I hardly recognized her, although I had seen her photograph many times—a lovely young girl with long hair and clear skin reflecting that well-groomed look so characteristic of affluent suburbia. But now her hair was cut severely short, her skin was pock-marked, and there was a gaunt solemnity about her face. She was studying a sheaf of papers as I said: "I'm Pat Bascio, and I have been looking forward to meeting you for years." As she looked up at my Roman collar she seemed to strain her eyes as if she were looking into a bright summer sun. She knew about me, she said, and we stood there holding each other's hands in a self-conscious interlude. I said: "It's almost lunch time; can I take you out for some lunch?'' Her awkwardness rivaled mine as she fumbled for a reply. I believe her "yes" was uncontrolled and even undesired, but that's how her nervousness articulated itself. I'm sure that if I had called her on the phone, the reply would have been negative. She would not have to look at my face as she said no. She put her reports in the wrong place, almost dropped them, as she tried to replace them in the proper slot. We walked out of the hospital without saying a word to each other, but she did begin to relax as we walked the streets making small talk about the weather and the profusion of garbage on the streets of Harlem. "Do you like Italian food? " I ventured, feeling a bit braver. She brightened up. "I love it." I knew a nice place a little farther downtown so I said, "Why not call the hospital and tell them you won't be back this afternoon, and we can spend the rest of the day together." I was as surprised as she to hear myself say this. After a long pause, she simply said, "O.K."

We were beginning to feel comfortable together as we entered the Italian restaurant. I ordered rigatoni with sausage for both of us and a chilled bottle of Italian wine. She asked me why I had become a priest. "To help the blacks," I said. She leaned back in her chair and laughed, but not meanly. "Do you really think you can help the blacks? What do you know about blacks or their problems? You priests are arrogant, just like the Pharisees. You come into the black community, relate to a mere handful of brainwashed, Uncle-Tom types, bless their rosaries, plan their baptisms, and offer words of superstitious consolation. What about all the others? What about the ninety percent? You don't know a damn thing about them and if you live here for fifty years you will never know about them because you mean nothing to them." I did not really seem to mind all this coming from

Patricia Sullivan. I guess it was because she was so openly honest and there was no sense of meanness, no irony. Between Pat and me there was developing right there and then an almost instant feeling of comradeship.

She began to speak about her childhood years and how she early-on sensed that she was different from her classmates and friends. Her girl friends enjoyed playing house, dressing dolls, and spending hours in fixing their hair. She had tried very hard to participate and enjoy all these activities but would invariably run away to be by herself. She had felt guilty about it, and worse than that, she was unable to fill the void left in her life by rejecting dolls, mother's high heels, and discarded and faded gowns. Gradually she became more and more isolated from the world of her peers, tried to analyze this self-imposed isolation as she grew into young womanhood, and became increasingly frustrated at her inability to come up with an answer. Her mother, a model of sophisticated femininity, enhanced by a delicate appreciation of music, art, and poetry that opened her up to the world, dealt with her in an understanding and loving manner.

Patricia looked in wonder at this world of her mother and envied the very patrician way in which she related to life around her and to her beloved Roman Catholicism. But Pat became increasingly disturbed at her mother's world, and she was unable to focus clearly on what exactly it was that disturbed her. Her thoughts seemed to come from deep inside her unconscious rather than from her intellect. Her own interest in the Church grew for a time as she sought an answer to the meaning of life and the purpose of existence. To her mother's surprise and delight, she attended Mass regularly and even participated in a parish retreat. But pray as she might, everything remained out of focus, and her mother asked her to pray for faith and enlightenment.

Entering nursing school gave her life, if not a voluntary and chosen direction, at least a disciplined routine which, combined with the obvious healing and life-supportive effects of the nursing profession, supplied some form and substance to her existence. Devotion to her patients became a reason for living and provided her with a fixed point of stability from which she now could make tentative gropings to the outside world.

An intensive study of her profession enhanced her growing awareness that she was called to a life of service to others. But who was calling her? Mom Sullivan assured her it was God, for only God inspired and motivated us to a life of service. In many quiet visits to empty churches and in the meditative repose that occurred in this setting, Patricia Sullivan felt she had a genuine experience of a divine presence speaking to her heart. Peculiarly, however, her desire for participation in the religious rites and practices of the Catholic Church seemed to diminish in direct ratio to the degree that her quiet conversations with the divine increased. She started seeing beyond the physical ailments of her patients to the economic stress that this caused in their families and loved ones. She began to wonder why the sick in our affluent society had to enter hospitals with the threat of financial disaster hanging over their heads. Her inquiries to several priests about the morality involved in the distribution of wealth and justice in our society left her with the uneasy feeling that the Church's evaluation of moral acts stopped at the boundary between personal and social actions. If the Church did not address itself to these problems, then did God? She thought about this for a long time and finally decided she had to go beyond the Christian acceptance of suffering and the Church's noninvolvement in the economic structure of society. She went back to talk to her divine presence in a small corner of her parish church and it told her that her destiny was to spend her life for the poor and disadvantaged.

Did this mean she would work for the change of our economic system? After all, how could the poor be assured of being able to have proper medical care unless the system was changed? He didn't answer on this point so she took silence as approval.

We had long finished our rigatoni as Pat recalled that at some point she irrevocably dismissed institutionalized religion as any longer meaningful to her and to the problems to which she addressed herself. Her decision was not made in anger and not even in criticism, just a feeling of irrelevance. But for a short period thereafter she continued to attend Mass and even an occasional Benediction with her mother in an effort to minimize the effects of what was eventually going to become an acute awareness on her mother's part that Pat no longer had the faith. At Benediction she wanted to pray for the destruction of an economic system that permitted the personal tragedies which she encountered every day in the hospital. At Mass she wanted to scream at the priest and prevent him from talking about visions and miracles and the potential evils of dating. What about the poor? What about the way the profit motive penalized the retarded, the nonaggressive, and the honest in our society? Why the hell didn't the priests address themselves to things that are substantial? It frustrated her and angered her and she wondered if the prophets had all ceased to exist after Jesus. She had heard of one priest who used to speak about social justice in a nearby town and who was now running a gas station near the Canadian border after having been silenced several times.

Then one day she was assisting a New York City doctor at an operation in Burlington and his language and concern seemed a reflection of her own. They met after the operation, went to dinner, and had a very long, and for Pat, fruitful conversation. He invited her to leave Burlington and work in Harlem, at Sydenham Hospital. There, he promised her, she would find others to whom she could relate, others who felt just as she did about the economic system and its damaging effects on the disadvantaged. It did not take her long to resign from her job, pack her bags, and leave for New York. There, her acquaintance with her doctor friend grew and led her to become a member of the Communist Party.

We left the Italian restaurant and there was no doubt that we had already become good friends. We walked for several hours, stopping every once in a while for a refreshing root beer at one of those many soft drink stands one finds on the streets of Manhattan. She was delighted we had met, she said, and only wished that we shared a common approach to human development. It would be a bit difficult to explain to the Party, she added, but would I join her the following evening? I forget exactly what the cause was but I do remember that it had something to do with South Africa, and the only thing I knew about South Africa at the time was that it was in the southern part of Africa. My attendance at this event turned out to be the first of innumerable encounters I was to have with Communists over the years. Of course, not many of them turned out to be as flexible and gentle as Patricia Sullivan. I found most of them to be rigid in their dogmatism, their unquestioning faith, and their narrowness of vision. They seemed to me to be the side of a coin having on its opposite side a similar portrait of the ultra-right-wing of the Catholic Church. I saw then and see now little difference between them. Of course, one could also see the similar dedication, singlemindedness, and determination that springs from this rigidity.

Pat was not rigid or dogmatic, but she was determined to work for what, in her view, was progressive change in the way our economy distributes its wealth. In the 1950's, people like Pat had little more to hang their ideas on than a few sprigs of hope, and she was a realist who knew that she would die without perhaps seeing any change whatsoever. Her courage and her lack of any personal ambition struck me so forcefully that for weeks I agonized over how this atheistic, cold, and rigid dogmatism could inspire such dedication and selflessness.

Pat called me at St. Mark's rectory about an hour before I was to meet her at Sydenham for the benefit. She pleaded with me not to wear my Roman collar, but I did anyway. Her fellow-workers at Sydenham knew her Communist affiliations, and they looked on with a mixture of amusement and incredulity as I walked up to her desk, took her by the arm, and escorted her out of the hospital. She said she would retaliate by showing up at St. Mark's the next day wearing a hammer and sickle armband and asking for her friend, Father Pat.

The concert at the Y.M.C.A. was a bore for me, a bad mixture of Richard Wagner and Mahler, hardly my favorite composers. The Party faithful turned out in large numbers, and there were definite signs of hostility and shock as Patricia, a popular member of the Party, introduced me around. She bravely continued introductions as the silence and coolness continued. At the end of the evening she admitted that there was little difference between her "faithful" in the matter of narrowness and the faithful of any other organization or institution.

I was scheduled to leave for East Africa in the fall, and Pat was increasingly involved in after-hours work with the Party so I saw little of her during the summer. But occasionally she would call me at St. Mark's about 10 p.m. and talk for an hour trying to interest me in making a study of Marxian socialism. The few pamphlets she gave me turned me off completely with their dry rhetoric and soulless analyses, so she made little progress with me, much to her disappointment.

Patricia Sullivan

Shortly before I sailed for East Africa, Pat extended what was her first invitation to have dinner at her apartment in the Village. It was as bare as a monk's cell; her eating utensils were made of rough wood, and her furniture could best be described as "second-hand." "Sorry I cannot provide you the comfort of your rectory," she said with a bit of friendly sarcasm, "but I give a percentage of my salary to the Party every week and that leaves me little for my own needs." There was no doubt in my mind about her sincerity or her integrity, and this alone was high praise for any person. I realized, perhaps more than she did, that each of us belonged to an international structure having many more similarities than the respective members would admit. I had already met many priests living in voluntary poverty and asking little for their own physical and emotional comfort. I guess I did not expect to find the same thing among Communists.

We corresponded while I was in Africa and my understanding of what she was and what gave her a worldview so radically different from mine began to grow and as it grew the ideological differences between us narrowed. As I discovered racism in myself and among my fellow Christians, the things Pat said to me in New York and the ideas she conveyed in her letters became more intelligible and more digestible in my consciousness. I came to Africa to "teach the natives" and discovered that they had so much more to teach me in the way of serenity, a natural affinity for the presence of God, a tolerance of the foreign, and an almost stoic but engaging acceptance of the will of God in life's fragile and sometimes almost tragically hard circumstances. "Shauri la Mungu," the Africans say in Swahili. "That's God's business." And along the roadways, in the shops, and in the marketplace the Africans greeted me with "Tumsifu Jesu Christu" — "praise be to Jesus Christ."

Their religious life permeated all of their daily acts and

there was no embarrassment or shyness about its expression. Rain, drought, near-starvation, racism, economic imperialism, loss of human dignity under colonial rule, the horror story of slavery—all absorbed in the seemingly infinite patience and wisdom of the African peoples. *Shauri la Mungu.* This was their answer to all of life's events. God seemed to permeate the air, the ground, the married life, the eating and drinking and dancing. It was a whole new experience for me. We came to preach the gospel in our seersucker suits and khaki shorts, supported by the whole logistical complex of electric lighting, refrigerators, cars, jeeps, Land Rovers, and money to buy whatever amenities we wanted as we lived in small islands of affluence in the midst of a sea of poverty. Life in Africa was, for some of us, the actualization of romantic seminary dreams rather than a serious interpenetration of our cultures and spiritual forces with theirs.

As I look back now, I see why the Africans laughed at us and yet they really did love us more than we had a right to be loved. They saw our shallowness, but we did not realize it. Like a mother absorbing the foolish fantasies and boasts of her children, they pressed us to their bosom and, if we permitted it, extended their love and tenderness to us. Seeing all this threw my whole worldview into confusion. I had come to teach and I had to declare myself incompetent in the face of the enormous integrity and strength I found all around me in the African environment. And most incredible of all was the capacity of the African to love the intruder, the plunderer, the paternalist. I will never cease to thank God for the enormous capacity of the black people to love their white brothers and sisters. It is one hope that the white world has for its salvation. Gradually, the whole mass of images, lessons, propaganda, impressions, yearnings, teachings as expressed by Patricia Sullivan began a slow but steady integration in my mind, leading to a subconscious awareness that my worldview was radically defective and immature. My simplistic notions of the interrelationships existing between nations and their respective cultures, economies, religion, and ambitions were based on an almost total ignorance of these factors. I realized that my seminary training in no way prepared me for the task of bringing Christ to the world. My naiveté, ignorance, superficiality, and lack of understanding almost crushed me. I lay on my bed one entire night overcome by frustration and mental disarray. In the morning I went to the chapel early and prayed to hold on to a faith which suddenly seemed supercilious, irrelevant, and dominated by white racism and pride. That day I walked through the local village, spending a few hours at the market observing the Africans and their way of life through different eyes, and knowing that I had to refashion all my thinking if I were to continue to feel a sense of integrity in my work. I also sensed that this new orientation, whatever form it would take, could cause great tensions with my fellow priests. And this, in fact, turned out to be the case.

For the next two years I took no positive direction but spent time silently observing myself, my confreres, the African peoples, and the host of interrelationships among all of us. My principal source of strength remained the connection with Patricia Sullivan, but it was a strength tinged with anxiety because I was not prepared to accept the possibility that any structure outside the Catholic Church could offer the Church any constructive advice on how to carry out its mission. But at the same time, I increasingly felt that I was part of a foreign force that dominated the economic, political, cultural, and religious life of the Africans and I became uneasy.

There had to be a change in myself. But how? to what?

The Rules and Constitution of my Religious Congregation were explicit regarding the kind of prayer life I should follow, the way I should carry out the various functions of my office, the rules of politeness and obedience due to my superiors, the human pitfalls and temptations that I should avoid. But what to do with the talents I had? how should I relate to the peoples to whom I was sent? what kind of contribution could I make, if any, in a foreign land? what should I know about the economic, political, cultural, and religious structures of the Africans? On these matters our Rules and Constitutions, our seminary training, the counseling of our superiors — all were silent. It was as if we had built a huge structure, as if each of us had been given a place in that structure, and that, all being ready for action, we had suddenly forgotten why it was we had gotten together in the first place and had forgotten just what it was this huge structure was supposed to accomplish.

Now I am being unfair because obviously we did build churches and schools, we did baptize, confess, and marry and give of our time and energy gladly and with generosity. And this alone was a magnificent example of the basic decency and good intentions motivating the Church; but my question was whether these, by themselves, were sufficient and proper tools for transforming the African condition from human and spiritual bondage to physical and spiritual freedom. I began to question everything, but I did the questioning silently because I had the greatest respect and affection for my fellow priests and our bishops. Their sacrifices and spirit of dedication was a fact of life which I experienced every day. And I suppose I was even wise enough to understand that I was too young in the priesthood to have acquired sufficient wisdom to make proper judgments.

I wrote to Patricia, expressing my doubts and frustrations. I expected she would write an "I told you so" sort of letter, but that was not Patricia Sullivan. Her reply was full of compassion and understanding and noticeably free of Communist rhetoric. It was just a letter from a friend who wanted to encourage and console. She said I should look at my newfound confusion as the throes of a new birth to a more mature understanding of myself, the world, and the black peoples of Africa. Her letter boosted my morale. It made me feel as if I had just discovered, after a long and tiring search, a new land. The length and the perils of the journey had exhausted me, but otherwise I was fine. Her letter carried me through what would have been a very bad period indeed. I knew I had to face the task of constructing an entirely new foundation for my faith, and for my work as a priest. I was frightened as to where this would lead me and I desperately wanted my new path not to lead me outside the Catholic Church. I was like the young man going off to the wars late at night and glancing back desperately at the warm glow of lights fading in the distance, yearning already to return to the love and security of his mother's embrace.

I knew that being a priest would never again be the same for me. The most agonizing aspect of my new-found isolation was my inability to communicate my feeling to my fellow priests. I now realize that I should have tried harder to make them listen. There were some emotionally taxing days ahead as a new consciousness and understanding of our role in Africa began to formulate in my mind. The stand I took in a dispute between my own superior and a group of African teachers soon embroiled me in a controversy, the effects of which still scar my relationship with some of my confreres. The anguish, crises of faith, lack of trust in me on the part of priests for whom I felt only the greatest affection, and the dislocation in my moral and religious judgments kept me on the verge of internal collapse. My correspondence with Patricia and the quiet moments spent in meditation in the school chapel kept me going and provided the encouragement and strength I needed for articulating my evolving thoughts.

I was happy when my tour of duty in Tanzania came to an end and I would be able to spend a period of re-evaluation at home, in an atmosphere that was part of me. Our plane arrived at Kennedy Airport (Idlewood then) at about nine in the evening, and I just felt so relaxed being in my own land again. I headed straight for a telephone. I wanted to thank Pat for the great help she had been to me during those months of personal crises.

But I did not get the opportunity. Her companion of many years tearfully told me of the great tragedy that had occurred in his life. Patricia Sullivan was dead from cancer. "Father Pat," this Communist found himself saying, "Patricia was the most beautiful and delicate of all God's creation." Both of us cried as he expressed his sorrow and loneliness.

In the dark of the Connecticut-bound limousine I recited prayers for the dead for Patricia Sullivan, a gentle Communist who had had such a profound effect on my life.

3
Thanksgiving at Dorothy Day's

Jonathan Bell was writing a paper on a problem having international implications. One day he was talking with a nun friend of mine in Brooklyn, and she suggested that since part of his paper dealt with the United Nations, he might like to get together with me for a chat. Jonathan called me at the rectory and we set up a meeting. It was the week before Thanksgiving and a very busy one for me, so we agreed that he would meet me early one morning and we would talk between appointments which I had in Brooklyn and Manhattan. We met at the Criminal Court building in Brooklyn at nine in the morning and parted about eight that evening in the delegates' lounge of the United Nations. Jonathan was interested in learning more about Third World attitudes toward nuclear disarmaments, world government, and economic development.

It turned out to my surprise and great delight that Jonathan was staying with Dorothy Day in the Bowery, so I took the opportunity to ask a lot of questions about her. Miss Day had been the folk-hero of many seminarians and priests in my seminary days, a symbol of loving and loyal dissent within the institutional Church. The influence of Dorothy Day on priests and nuns in thousands of communities across this land can never be measured because

Dorothy Day is not an institutional person and does not keep records or statistics on such things. Many of us knew, instinctively, that in this lady were reflected the highest ideals of, and the most radical conformity to, the person and teachings of Jesus Christ. Her stands against war and in favor of the Church's commitment to the relief of the downtrodden were thorns in the sides of clergy and laity who patriotically supported "just wars" and who enjoyed the fruits of unrestricted capitalism. Her fearless and radical views caused uneasiness in rectories and chancery offices from coast to coast. Many of the clergy who perhaps felt threatened by her unorthodox views were quick to dissociate themselves from her. Because she had no constituency, sought no ecclesiastical positions or favors, avoided the arena of religious politics, and busied herself with the essentials of the Christian message, she was much freer to address herself to moral issues than were the clergy, whose institutional ties and bonds restricted their ability to speak out openly about the liberating message of Jesus.

The institutionalization of the Church has led it, perhaps inevitably, to shed its role as prophet and to assume, more often than has been good for the people of God, the mantle of defender of the established government and institutions. I do not mean to play the role of critic here because I do not see how it can be different. You would have to live in the clerical world to understand the need for compromise in the real world of building churches, collecting funds, keeping parishioners happy and bishops and superiors contented. It is a balancing act in which there is no way to avoid personal compromise. I'm not saying this is bad because we cannot live in society without give and take; I'm only saying that this is a fact. Developing programs for the poor and the disenfranchised in a socio-economic milieu that rewards the clever, the

Thanksgiving at Dorothy Day's 31

well-educated, and the ambitious, is politically unwise and can lead to the abrupt demise of a promising career. Dorothy Day had no one to please except Jesus Christ. She said that war was evil and that the working man and his unions should be defended. She said the poor and the disenfranchised should be the object of loving care by the institutional Church. She was called a Communist by those who associate the equitable distribution of a society's wealth with atheistic communism. Dorothy Day had no investments, not even in herself, so there was nothing to lose. Her position was unassailable and free from the temptations to power and compromise. Of course, the devil is a busy guy so I am sure she had other and more subtle temptations.

There is one terrible temptation which afflicts those who work among God's poor, a temptation with which Dorothy Day may have had many a tryst. It is the feeling that you are doing the *real* work of the Lord and the rest of the do-gooders are working for their own benefit. This insidious temptation must be fought at every turn and great vigilance must be exercised to detect its presence. This is especially true since the very desire and vocation to work among the disenfranchised is itself an inspiration from and a gift of God and has nothing to do with one's native abilities or magnanimity. Such a gift is all too easily corrupted by pride and arrogance, so a self-reminder of the origin of all gifts and prophecies is vitally important.

I remember a particular Saturday evening in East Africa sitting alone next to my *fanusi* (lamp) and thinking about those lucky fellows at home going out to football games after a couple of hours of confessions. Since I wanted to be at Notre Dame stadium myself, I wondered if I were any more dedicated to my missionary vocation than were the priests at the stadium that evening. Human beings are fragile and complicated. Our need to project ourselves favorably to the world is so strong that one wonders how many truly selfless acts proceed from an inner core of self-giving and how many proceed from drives that are basically self-serving. Only God knows and God is too sensitive to our pride to discourage us with the truth. The fellow who gives up a life of marriage to care for his mother and the woman who lives with a drunken husband are often more self-giving than the professional do-gooders. Those who are professionally dedicated to the service of the poor can only hope that they will develop the integrity and holiness of these ordinary people.

But whatever temptations Dorothy Day may have experienced as a result of her special vocation, there is sufficient evidence to support the conclusion that she has mightily resisted them. Her commitment is backed by a voluntary life of poverty and a daily sharing with many who are difficult to associate with. There is a wide gap between writing a check for the poor from behind a walnut desk and eating and living with the outcasts and derelicts of our society.

After Jonathan and I had spent the day together, he suggested to Dorothy Day that I might be invited to the Thanksgiving Day meal at her place in the Bowery and then called me at the rectory in Brooklyn and informed me of the invitation. This opportunity to meet Miss Day and to share Thanksgiving Day with her and her friends delighted me no end. As I prepared to meet with her, I ran over in my mind the possible subjects we might get to discuss if she had the time. I wondered if we would talk about the use of violence. She is a passionate believer in nonviolence, insisting that peaceful and persistent efforts to effect change are not merely suggested by the teachings of Christ but are demanded by them. This is a problem that haunts all people of good will in the Third World who see the necessity for structural changes, but who live in a society which is unwilling to change outmoded and repressive structures and to this end use the power of the police state.

As I have suggested elsewhere, we are badly in need of a theology of violence. I hope it does not come too late for the Church to play a role in the dramatic and rapid changes taking place throughout the world. In some areas of the world it is already too late. In Southeast Asia and parts of the African continent, resistance to structural changes has resulted in the formation of Marxist-Leninist revolutions. Perhaps in the Caribbean, South America, and Western Europe there is barely enough time to inform structural changes with the saving power of Jesus Christ, but it hardly seems possible that the Church can adapt itself to this huge task in the time left. We appear destined to lose our opportunity to change the face of the earth.

Since violence involves the use of force, can we not distinguish between one who uses force to violate another person and one who uses force to repel such a violation? Could we not define violence as the *unjust* use of force? I know that the theologians will respond: "Well, once you allow *any* use of force, then who is to say what is just and what is unjust?" This argument betrays a laziness of spirit, a lack of theological expertise and common sense, and a lack of trust that the gospel message of Christ will give us the answer. After all, that is precisely why Christ went through all the trouble of being born and dying on the cross. He wanted to give us the answers to the problems of life so that we could act freely and surely as we went about building the human city with the mind of God. A meditation on the gospel message will lead us to choose between right and wrong in even the most difficult moral dilemmas. To say that we Christian adults will not be able to distinguish between just and unjust use of force is to deny the usefulness of the teaching Church and to betray an absence of that boldness of spirit which was reflected by Christ when he said that he had come to cast fire upon the earth.

Miss Day's dining room-kitchen was crowded as we entered on Thanksgiving Day. A lady with wild, wide eyes and straggly hair welcomed us and produced an orange crate for me to sit on. I turned it over to Joan Latapy, who had accompanied me.

Joan is from Success Village, in the outskirts of Port-of-Spain, Trinidad. She is the mother of three boys and was working as a domestic in Manhattan, and in her spare time she did a lot of my typing connected with United Nations work. Although Joan had only gone to primary school, her street experience in Trinidadian politics made her invaluable to me in matters dealing with the sensitivities and aspirations of Third World nations, especially in the Caribbean. Joan is outgoing, spontaneous in her joy, and a very compassionate person. Once, as I was rushing to the United Nations from 125th Street for an appointment, she made me stop the car as she spotted a wounded pigeon who had flown right smack into the side of an apartment building. It took her about an hour to attend to his wounds and drop him off at a friend's apartment where the pigeon would be nursed until it was able to be airborne once again. I was late for my appointment and Joan's only comment was: "You really could not have left that pigeon out on the street, could you?" There was no answer to that logic.

We had hardly been at Miss Day's for half an hour and Joan had already become the center of a group of disheveled men and women, her neatly-rounded Afro bobbing excitedly in a sea of unkemptness. Her West Indian accent fascinated the group, and one lady, who had evidently seen better days, spoke of memories of balmy nights and soft sea breezes during Caribbean cruises, long

Thanksgiving at Dorothy Day's 35

ago. Something struck me as I watched Joan forming her spontaneous island of joy among a group which had already arrived at various levels of psychological and physical deterioration. I noticed that there seemed to be an absence of gaiety in the room. Dorothy Day sat at a table in the midst of her friends, chatting softly with each and attending to their needs, but there was a lack of joy and spontaneity in her face and this surprised me. The young people who waited on tables reflected this same somber expression. No doubt they were intense and dedicated, but a lightness of spirit and some laughter would have made all the difference to the atmosphere of that room. I have rarely found a genuine outpouring of Christian love and dedication in people who do not laugh. Joan Latapy, who feels uncomfortable in a Church unless it is empty, but who radiates love and innocent playfulness, was the only really bright spot in the rather depressing atmosphere.

One of the young helpers came over to tell me that Miss Day was busy at the moment sharing her meal with the visitors, but would be able to talk to me in a little while. Jonathan Bell kept me company and Joan was busy expanding her circle of new-found friends. Jonathan took up where we had left off the day we spent together. We had been discussing the "system." I argued that an economic system which rewarded the talented, the shrewd, the unscrupulous, and the greedy, and neglected the retarded, the shy, the aged, and the nonaggressive, needed some moral and structural changes. Television reports claimed that the elderly of New York City were resorting to purchasing dog and cat food for their own consumption because they could not afford to purchase regular cuts of meat. Jonathan acknowledged that there were inequities in the society, but he was frightened by the prospect of structural changes, fearing that this would inevitably lead to either communism or a dictatorship or both. He explained that once one starts on the road to serious change, there is no turning back. His solution to the problems of our society was to modify the system to make it more humane and more responsive to human needs and more aware of and compassionate toward human tragedies.

This sounds good, but the question is, is it possible? Can you have an economic system based on the maximization of profits which can be motivated to remove the very conditions which are the *sine qua non* of its continued existence? Can you obliterate surplus labor without obliterating the entrepreneur? Would not the capitalist system that produces the kind of surplus labor that enriches the entrepreneur continue in employer-employee relationships and would not this deterioration eventually bring about, in the Marxist sense, class conflict? Has this not been happening in the world around us, and are we immune? Was not the history of labor-management relations in America, especially in the formation of the big unions, a classic case of class conflict? The power of the big labor unions evolved only after prolonged strikes and violence in American society. Jonathan maintained that there is no such thing as class conflict, that this was a myth invented by Marx. Is Jonathan correct or is this not the typical response of those who attempt to make conditions in the real world resemble the abstract world of the theoretical model of the classical economist? This can be dangerous business, because the classical economists pressure governmental bodies to continue social conditions which will maintain, by force, the classic economic model regardless of the changing production relationships that occur in the real world. Translated into political terms, this requires the emergence of political dictatorships such as we have witnessed in South Korea and

Chile. In the end, the attempt will prove futile, for to continue an economic or social model long after it has already died is to court social unrest and to open the door to extremists of both the right and the left.

In this country the preservation of outmoded social concepts is exemplified in the question of guaranteed quality medical care for all Americans. In some quarters, it is held as a dangerous, even revolutionary idea, that all American citizens should have a right to low-cost medical care. Exactly why it is harmful, dangerous, and even revolutionary, no one ever exactly explains, least of all the poor, the disadvantaged, and those living on Social Security income. But the idea, aided and abetted by the American Medical Association, persists in our society. It persists even in the face of horrendous and economically disastrous hospital costs and doctors' fees.

I also observed to Jonathan that, in my view, the surest guarantee of bringing on ourselves the type of government which he so feared was to continue to hide our heads in the sand. One day it is going to occur to a majority of Americans that it is obscene that a Frank Sinatra should get thousands of dollars for a week's work. We are courting violent public unrest with this kind of disparity between the wages of people who, after all, are fundamentally of the same nature and each of whom makes a different but socially equal contribution to what becomes the totality of our society. It is a kind of madness we have acquired in the West and as a result the Socialist countries have plenty of material to feed into their propaganda machines all over the world, courtesy of our economic system and its ridiculous inconsistencies.

Jonathan could agree with most of what I said, but he stopped short of agreeing that we should campaign to do anything concrete about the problems. I can understand his attitude, after all, that what we have seen happen in nations where social unrest, even with the best intentions on the part of those who foment it, has often led to chaos in the economy and to the disturbing of social peace and harmony. But is it not also true that the longer we wait the more uncertain our future will be? Is it possible for us to look at changes in Italy, Portugal, Guyana, Jamaica, and France and not realize that something of a very big order is taking place out there beyond our shores, something which is going to have a profound effect on the lives of the next generation? Should we not begin a great public debate on how we can, in a democratic manner, rid ourselves of pornography, excessively wide disparities in income, and the shame of the rapid deterioration of the main urban centers of America, where most of our people live and work? Is it necessary to wait until we reach the point where the job may be done undemocratically? If we had backed democratic and just governments in Vietnam and other places around the world, would not some of those nations now living under totalitarian rule instead be basking in the sun of democratic government? What further human tragedies do we need to make us move!

Dorothy Day finished her meal with her friends, joined them in washing dishes, and then sat with Joan and me for a chat. I had expected her to speak with a kind of unguarded openness, but she did not. Perhaps it was all those difficult years, the opposition, the disappointments, and the mistrust. But as we talked, I felt I was listening to someone who possessed a closed mind. Perhaps she is simply getting old and has become rooted in a rhetoric that is of her past. But whatever the cause, there seemed no possibility of dialogue but only irritation at ideas not consonant with her own. I explained that while I appreciated her devotion to those who became misfits in a system that rewards the strong, another approach, and a more important approach, would be to work toward the changing of that system. This may have struck her as cruel or as unappreciative, but it was not intended to be so. One could only disagree with Dorothy Day with the greatest caution and reverence, being mindful that the saints have a wisdom that transcends academia. I guess my approach was wrong and certainly my ideas did not please her, and our conversation soon came to an end. It was a great disappointment to me that I did not get the opportunity to discuss a wide range of issues with someone who had thought and prayed about the most important problems of our time and it has given me pause to wonder about the correctness of my own views. But I did sit with Dorothy Day on Thanksgiving Day and for that privilege I shall always be thankful.

4
A Christian Response to Marxism?

When this century has run its course and historians and social commentators begin to reflect on the particular contribution it made to the world, there is little doubt that its main feature and characteristic will be that the restructuring of the social order has begun. And it will be noted that the guiding and motivating force behind this very radical, though gradual, development did not proceed from the institutions established for that purpose but from maverick men and women and maverick institutions. The evolving social consciousness which is the motivating force for change came, not from the research departments of the world's great universities, nor from the well-planned conferences of government officials, but rather from the scattered but increasingly united interactions which take place daily in the marketplace between the managers of industry and the working people. Marx called these interactions the class struggle. In any given society, the striving of some of its members conflicts with the striving of others. The conflicting strivings originate from the difference in the position and life-style of the classes into which each society is divided. "The history of all hitherto existing societies is the history of class struggles." Interestingly enough, Engels later added that this is true except for the so-called "primitive societies." Anyone who has worked in tribal Africa will concur with Engels, for the African tribal structure is based on communal rather than hierarchical social interaction. For example, the chief's hut is indistinguishable from anyone else's. Representative institutions, universal suffrage, inexpensive daily press, and powerful unions, all have sprung from the tension between the haves and have nots in Western society.

Another way to express what has been happening in this century is that humankind has decided to put aside the gods and superstitions that have been in control of our destiny and has taken a position in the very center of the universe. We did this without support from our religious institutions since we were forbidden to do so (as Galileo and others discovered) on the grounds that such a realignment was dangerous and inimical to salvation. It also violated the philosophical idealism of the ages, which has always resisted any transition from idealism to realism. The democratic Western concepts of liberty, equality, and fraternity somehow got stuck in a Platonian ideal world, and every effort to concretize the democratic ideals was somehow frustrated by more religious and social idealism. So the proponents of change looked elsewhere. They drew their inspiration from a body of historical knowledge and experience that conformed neither to the prior construction of idealism nor the academic niceties of high institutions of learning. Shedding the myths and superstitions of their ancestors, they began to find, in the concrete physical reality of daily living, the meaning of life. They began to see human living as intending goals and responding to values that flow from human interaction, as guiding means to ends, not allowing itself to become a controlled ripple reflected off the vast uncontrollable sea of human destiny. Human living with its social interactions constitutes social systems and adorns them with cultural expressions. It transforms the world of individuals as they explode in all their unique articulateness, lavishly creating and fashioning a hierarchy of goals. Human beings humanize themselves. Their history is the process of self-realization. Contrary to the popular interpretation of Marx which has him liberating human beings by divorcing them from their own history, Marx insisted that "men make their own history, but they do not do it exactly as they please . . . but under circumstances directly encountered, given and transmitted from the past" ("The Eighteenth Brumaire of Louis Bonaparte," Marx and Engels, *Selected Works* [Moscow, 1969], Vol. I, p. 247).

While the Church, state, and university continued to refine, support, rationalize, and enhance the classical social, economic, and cultural model, the person in the street has been undergoing social, economic, and cultural conversion. To the academic potpourri of highly stylized propositions of the classicist, the proletariat has opposed the highly volatile ingredients of the meanings and values of human interactions.

> Society is the fulfilled unity of man with nature, the actual resurrection of nature, the perfect naturalization of man and the perfect humanization of nature [Marx, *Historische Materialismus*, Kroner ed., I, 297].

In contrast to the static view of history as a nonevolutionary repetition of a limited number of human cycles, Marx saw history in its development toward a period of final perfection via a period of distortion after a fall from original perfection. The idea of a universal goal of history connects Marxian interpretation of history with

A Christian Response to Marxism? 43

the prophetic one and distinguishes it from those interpretations of history in which the universal direction is denied and the meaning of history is explained in the growth and decay of nations, races, and cultures. Marx, unconsciously, comes very close here to defining the role of God working in history. His is a prophetic, antimechanistic interpretation of history which declares that if humans are shaped by circumstances, circumstances must be shaped humanly. Marx's view of history is pre-eminently and profoundly religious, and it is obvious that he was greatly influenced by the Jewish and Christian heritage, far more influenced by it than many Christians turned out to be. Marx's messianism places him in secular attire among the great prophets of Israel and Christianity.

Christianity and Marxism. I do not see them as antagonists, as "us" and "them." I see two ideologies both striving to solve the problems of people-in-the-world. There are no good guys and bad guys. There are only people trying to come to grips with a world in flux. Marx has made his contribution, a great contribution, but the problems persist; alienation is no respector of ideologies.

Is there hiding in some obscure corner of the living Church a solution to the problems of people-in-the-world? Perhaps somewhere in the volumes of papal encyclicals, discourses, and allocutions a seed can be found which when planted and nurtured can revive an increasingly irrelevant Christian scholarship. The Encyclical *Mater et Magistra* contains such a seed.

Socialium rationum incrementa
Socialis vitae incrementa
Socialium rerum progressus

These expressions, found in the encyclical, sent shudders through the collective spine of millions of traditionalists throughout the Catholic world. Here was a pope of the Roman Catholic Church mentioning a bad word in the religious lexicon. The term "socialization" was casually used and defined without fear by the man whom many Catholics regard not only as the conservator of the Faith of our Fathers, but also the symbol of the strength and durability of conservative capitalism. And beyond that, the contrast between this presentation of the Church's social teaching and that of Pope Pius XII was not at all encouraging to the traditionalist. Pius, in a radio broadcast to the Congress of Austrian Catholics, warned:

> The person and the family must be saved . . . from an all-embracing socialization.

So, here was one pope advocating socialization and another condemning it. Confusion. However, John XXIII did not see this task as juxtaposing his social concepts with those of Pius XII, but rather of describing "one of the most chacteristic features of our age." In any case, there was nothing in his encyclical that directly contradicted the teachings of Pius XII. John XXIII was referring, not to nationalization nor state control of production and distribution of goods and services, but rather to the growing interdependence between peoples which is both a condition for and a consequence of social groupings. John added a growing eschatological dimension to the social teaching of the Church which does not focus on the apocalypse but rather looks to the gospel message as providing an atmosphere in which the divine presence in the world will facilitate and catalyze the dawning of a new age. I have no doubt that Pope John understood that the phenomenal success of Marxist socialism has to be essentially connected with earthbound eschatological yearnings. The eschaton is here and now. Pope John was not

A Christian Response to Marxism? 45

describing a merely political process but a cultural change which expresses itself in an irresistible human urge to join with others in achieving human goals that cannot be achieved by the spirit of rugged individualism. Recent papal encyclicals have come a long way toward accepting the Marxist analysis of history and a long way from the sentiments of Pope Pius X:

> In the order of human society as established by God there are rulers and ruled, employers and employees, rich and poor, learned and ignorant, nobility and proletariat [Pius X, "Fin dalla Prima," Dec. 18, 1903, Motu Proprio on Catholic Action].

Our tenaciously held conviction that individual freedom can be attained only within the economic system of unrestricted capitalism so limits our ability to deal with the problems in our society that we appear determined to let the whole structure fall down around us rather than explore cultural and economic alternatives. We need to liberate ourselves from this self-imposed imprisonment. The crime rate and the immersion of our society and culture in pornography are but two of the many social ills which resist solution precisely because too many of us are hiding behind the First Amendment in order to carry out, in the name of rugged individualism, acts and policies which are destroying the moral fiber of our nation and of Western society.

We must impose some restrictions on ourselves. The kind of restriction to the freedom of the individual of which the Pontiff speaks flows naturally from the experience of interdependence. A husband and wife voluntarily limit their freedom for sexual contact to preserve the dignity of their partner and the integrity of their marriage. We were not meant to be completely free. This is also recognized by the proponents of unrestricted capitalism, but in the capitalist society it takes the form of the protection of private property by the police power of the state. The question of freedom is, to some extent, a straw dummy because the real issue is what we do with our freedom. Do we use it to maintain the rugged individualism which crushes the poor, the ignorant, and the retarded, or do we use our freedom to structure our interdependence in such a manner as to distribute the fruits of our labors with equity and compassion? John XXIII affirmed that people can modify and shape social reality in accordance with action freely taken under the guidance of a conscience informed by the teachings of the gospel. To safeguard the socially conscious liberty of the individual, John implicity invokes the principle of subsidiarity. First, the increasing role of the state is an inevitable result of socialization and, secondly, authentic communities formed by increasing socialization must "treat their individual members as persons, and encourage them to take an active part in their own affairs." The Pope calls for a balance among the freedom of movement, action of individuals and groups, and the coordination and direction of the private sector by the state.

   The socialization of Karl Marx is, at least theoretically, being applied in many nations throughout the world. The socialization of Pope John has yet to be applied in even one nation. If the prospect of socialization without a soul is not to become a reality, we must raise our voices in prophecy and take affirmative action. The implementation of the social teachings of the Church is the task of all. This is the challenge. I try to be optimistic.

5
Marxism, Communism, and communism: The Difference

> *There can be no doubt that between capitalism and communism there lies a definite transition period, . . . between capitalism which has been defeated but not destroyed and communism which has been born but is still very feeble* [Lenin].

The first and most important step one must take in discussing Marxism with pious and intelligent Christians of goodwill is to make the all-important distinction between Marxism and communism. No intelligent or informative dialogue can take place on the subject of Marxism unless this is first established. In the mind of most Christians, more especially in the United States, which has not experienced the widespread adherence to Marxist principles now taking place among Christians in Europe, Africa, and Latin America, Marxism and communism are convertible terms. Nothing could be further from the truth.

However, it is easy to understand how this confusion came to be. The spread of Marxist principles throughout the world (in roughly the last fifty years), the acceptance of Marxism in Eastern Europe, all of this has taken place, politically, in those nations which have declared themselves "Communist." And so we have come to identify Communist with "communist" or with "Marxist." But the fact is that there is no such thing as a communist country now existing anywhere in the world, and in many countries now called Communist, many Marxists would not wish to live. In Marxist terms, the nations which have declared themselves "Communist" are only on the threshold of the change from capitalism to socialism to communism, since the transformation of a capitalist state to a truly communist state is a process that takes much longer than a mere fifty years, perhaps more than two or three hundred years. The development of human beings from the capitalist mentality to the communist mentality is an evolution of such magnitude that the dialectical process which shall bring it about has only just begun. Lenin said:

> What is usually called socialism was termed by Marx the "first" or lower phase of communist society. Insofar as the means of production become common property, the word "communism" is also applicable here, providing we do not forget that this is not complete communism [*Lenin* (Moscow: Progress Publishers, 1973), p. 345].

People change very slowly. The deep-rooted capitalist mentality must first undergo radical transformation, and a real moral conversion is necessary. The moral conversion is difficult to come by since the Church and the state have succeeded in labelling Marxism as evil and, until recent times, has upheld modern Western cultural capitalism as the embodiment of freedom and of Christian values. Obviously if Marxism is declared an evil by the Church then to suggest that one must undergo a moral conversion in order to comprehend communism is to talk heresy and nonsense. This excommunication has in the past effectively removed the possibility of academic enquiry into the value of Marx's principles. Even when, as has happened in the Catholic nations of Cuba, Italy, France, and Chile, a conversion takes place and capitalism is rejected in theory, the declaration of adherence to socialist principles is, by itself, only skin deep.

What we have to deal with here is a communist society, not as it has developed on its own foundations, but on the contrary, just as it *emerges* from capitalist society; which is thus in every respect, economically, morally and intellectually, still stamped with the birth marks of the old society from whose womb it emerges [*The Karl Marx Library*, (New York: McGraw-Hill, 1971) Vol. 1, p. 495].

Since the transformation of a capitalist state to a communist state can only begin after a very long period of socialism and since we are only on the threshold of socialism, we can see that not only is there no such thing as a communist state in existence today but also that it is not likely that even our children's grandchildren shall ever get so much as a glimpse at one. Communist countries have made only the first hesitant steps in the direction away from capitalism. This led Lenin to say that communism in its first phase retains "the narrow horizon of bourgeois law." By this he meant that the bourgeois state apparatus, since it cannot change overnight as by a miracle, remains fully intact during the early stage of communism even without the presence of the bourgeoisie.

This may appear to be a paradox unless one has experienced such a sociological phenomenon at first hand. In the British West Indies, for example, there still exists a strong British colonial influence in dress, food, and education even though in some cases the British have been gone from the local scene for at least twenty years. Strong anticolonial harangues are often shouted out under the tropical sun in heavy British accents by black leaders dressed in heavy woolen suits. Certainly anyone familiar with the Irish has experienced the vehement anti-British tirades coming from the Irish whose greatest pride is that they can speak the English language and that they have almost succeeded in imitating the best British accent, at the best British universities.

The same sociological pattern can be seen in societies opting for socialism while retaining, for a very long period of time, the capitalist mind-structure. The aberrations, purges, and intraparty struggles that have taken place in Communist states are partly explained by the intensity of the reaction against hundreds of years of oppression and sometimes inept efforts to develop a society, the model for which has never existed.

> The confusion of ends and means that led Stalin . . . to proclaim that socialism had been established . . . could only happen in a country where capitalism had never achieved . . . complete integration [Roger Garaudy, *The Alternative Future* (New York: Simon and Schuster, 1974)].

Marxism is future-look. The legacy of Marx is in part the desire to challenge the past, to cut out the dead wood of outmoded societal forms, and to create a new society. The greatest prophet of them all would not have disagreed:

> I have come to bring fire to the earth, and how I wish it were blazing already! [Luke 12:49].

The legacy of Marx is not Communism, but communism, a futurable. Communism is the transcendence of

Marxism, Communism, and communism 51

capitalism through transformation of its structure. The structural transformation that communism strives for strikes at the three principal bases of the capitalist system: labor, land, and money. Labor must no longer be subject to a contract between two unequal parties. Land must be removed from the market-place. When the laborer is no longer subject to a contract between two unequal parties, he is asserting the possibility of his own liberation.

The liberation of the workers will be accomplished by the workers themselves [Marx].

Those who are directly involved must be the principal agents of their own advancement [John XXIII].

And, happily, these three bases of the capitalist system have been under steady scrutiny by papal encyclicals in recent times. This leads us to an exciting possibility. It may not be the Communists who bring communism to its fruition. It may not even be the Marxists. After all, although the disciples of Jesus Christ have preached peace and justice since the star appeared over Bethlehem, it was not Christianity that brought peace and justice to the colonized and ravaged lands that suffered under both colonialism and imperialism. Honesty requires us to ask: has it not been the Marxists—Fidel Castro, Mao Zedong, Ho Chi Minh, and Che Guevara—who have fought for the dignity of the common person. It is a sad commentary on the institutional Church that the motivation for their liberation struggles came not from the Christian Churches but from Karl Marx. The truth is that the Christian Churches opposed every one of these men.

Of course, Marxists are also made of flesh and blood, and history has a way of repeating itself. Just as the institutionalization of the gospel message caused a paralysis of its dynamism, idealism, and sanctity, so the progressive institutionalization of Marxist regimes and policies may result in strangers grabbing the fire from their hands and carrying it forth into future history. The day of communism, if it should ever arrive, is too far into the future to say now how it will come about. Its present disciples may betray its message and lose its charism:

> Then the Master said to his servant, "Go to the open roads, and the hedgerows and force people to come in to make sure my house is full; because I tell you, not one of those who were invited shall have a taste of my banquet" [Luke 14: 22–24].

The Castros, Mao Zedongs, and Che Guevaras were not among those who were invited to the Master's house. They were picked up on the open roads and hedgerows and forced (inspired) to carry out at a certain period of time in history the plan of God for humankind's journey into the future, a time that saw the lack of such leadership and inspiration from the hierarchy and clergy of the Christian Churches. By the same token, it may be the Christian communities of the future who complete the task of communism. Maurice Bishop, the Prime Minister and former Black Power leader on the island nation of Grenada in the West Indies, once confided to me on the veranda of his house:

> We are struggling to bring about a revolutionary change in the social structures of West Indian society. Perhaps we will die in this struggle. And perhaps my own son will grow up to be a counterrevolutionary.

Just as Karl Marx, an atheist, reignited the social conscience of the Christian West, so communism may be brought to its full development not by the disciples of Marx but by a converted Christianity. This may sound like mere poetry but it could happen. Marxism is the socio-political worldview espoused and developed by Karl Marx. His writings are numerous, sometimes ponderous, sometimes bitterly comical and outrageous, but always brilliant and incisive. Marxism is not a political doctrine, but it does have almost frightening political implications:

> Let the ruling classes tremble at a communist revolution. The proletarians have nothing to lose but their chains. They have a world to win. Workingmen of all countries, unite! [*The Communist Manifesto*].

Marxism becomes a political doctrine when a group within a capitalist society (or any other societal form) decide that they would like to construct an economic system based on the writings of Karl Marx. Marxism is not an ideological doctrine, but the ideological implications become evident when Marx either analyzes the evils of the capitalist system or extols the virtues of communism. His eloquence is matched only by that of the prophets:

> The bourgeoisie has left remaining no other nexus between man and man than naked self-interest, than callous 'cash payment'. It has drowned the most heavenly ecstasies . . . in the icy water of egotistical calculation [*The Karl Marx Library*, Vol. 1, p. 503].

Marx's incisive socio-economic insights are often accompanied by the prophet's characteristic display of uncontrollable anger as he cries out against the injustices of an economic system so devoutly and stoutly defended by the religious and political institutions of capitalist society.

If Marxism means anything at all it can only mean the

writings and personal life-witness of Karl Marx. Marx drew together the three main ideological currents of the nineteenth century: classical German philosophy (Ludwig Feuerbach and Friedrich Hegel), classical English political economy (Adam Smith and David Ricardo), and French socialism (Saint Simon and Fourier). He was especially influenced by Feuerbach's materialism (which he criticized for not being sufficiently consistent) and Hegelian dialectics, which he considered the greatest achievement of classical German philosophy. As Marx saw it, Hegel's writings contained the philosophical underpinnings of a truly historical understanding of the development and evolution of humankind. Lenin was attracted to this dialectical approach to nature as he studied Marx, and he saw the discovery of radium, electrons, and the like as proof that nature's process is dialectical and not metaphysical, thereby confirming the legitimacy of Marx's incarnation of Hegelian idealism. For both Marx and Engels, the world was not to be understood as a complex of ready-made things but a complex of processes, an uninterrupted change of coming into being and passing away. The dialectical philosophy of Marxism proclaims that nothing is final or absolute; everything is transitory, everything passes away. The basic spirituality of this approach to nature and to the world cannot escape the reader of religious literature:

> You brush men away like waking dreams;
> they are like grass sprouting,
> and flowering in the morning,
> withered and dry before dusk.
> . . . Our lives are over in a breath [Psalm 90].

Marx's affinity with Judeo-Christian ideas and spirituality is so evident that I personally have never been able to understand why it is that Christians have such an abhorrence for Marx or why it is that Marxists can speak disrespectfully of Jesus Christ. For both Christ and Marx, the poor shall inherit the earth. It seems to me totally unfair to blame either Christ or Marx for the human aberrations of their followers. Both Christ and Marx have been, and continue to be, betrayed by their disciples.

Communism (capital C), in contrast to communism (small c), is a political system which has declared allegiance to the socio-economic principles imbedded in the works of Marx. This political system, as historical events themselves have testified, has too often been marked by the same brutality, lust for power, and disregard for human dignity that has characterized the Christian governments which it has replaced. But communism (in contrast to Communism) is not a political system; it is a way of life, a posture in the world. Lenin warned his compatriots that they must distinguish between what had universal validity in the Russian Revolution and what was specifically Russian. It was the mistaken theorization on the basis of this contingent model that caused Soviet tanks to be sent into Budapest. To call the Stalin regime Marxist and to mean by this that Stalin's political and personal life-style was a by-product of Marxist theory, is like saying that the life-style and political obscenities of the Borgias were a mirror-reflection of Christ, whose principles they publicly espoused. And just as the charitable and religious works of countless Christians continued to occur and develop during the Borgia regimes, so the ordinary Russian peasant continued to build a new socio-economic system based on Marx during the most excessive of Stalin's mental and political obscenities.

The Communist Revolution that took place in Russia is not the communist revolution. While a change of structures is a *sine qua non* for the passing from capitalism to communism, it is not enough. People must also change. The change from private ownership to nationalized ownership which took place in the Soviet Union was a structural change necessary to move toward communism, but the transfer of power from the Czar to the Communist Party has been of value only to the extent that the Communist Party in Russia has been true to its self-declared aim of moving in the direction of communism. If the alienation against authority is replaced by the alienation from the authority of the Communist Party, then communism may be advanced structurally (and this is a good in itself) but the overall good which should result may not be visible for a very long period of time.

Oscar Wilde, who certainly was never accused of being a card-carrying Communist, understood the distinction between Communism and communism. He dreamt of "a socialist or communist regime that would transform property into public wealth [and] would substitute cooperation for competition." It is quite possible that the communism of Karl Marx shall prove to be more an ideal to be sought after than a way of life which will in fact become universally adopted. "Be perfect as your heavenly Father is perfect" was a universal goal enunciated by Christ 2,000 years ago, and even a brief look at the history of the Christian West since that time hardly even remotely suggests that such a condition of perfection shall ever be realized on this earth.

"Sir, was it not good seed that you sowed in your field?. . . Do you want us to go and weed it [the chaff] out?" But he said, "No, because when you weed out the chaff you might pull up wheat with it. Let them both grow till the harvest" [Matthew 13:24–30].

Communists then are not those who live under the condition of communism. They are, rather, those who yearn for and struggle for the eventual historical coming-to-be of communism. In much the same way a Christian today is not someone who lives in a state or society whose life-style reflects the gospel message of Jesus Christ, since no Christian society exists today, but one who yearns for and struggles for such a blessed condition. Perhaps the Christian is a bit less optimistic than the Communist, since Christianity has been with us for 2,000 years and just under the skin lie our still primitive urges and weaknesses. Two thousand years of preaching the Christian message has produced countless numbers of heroic Christians but not one decent Christian state. The new human being may have emerged, but not the new society. It now remains to be seen if the Marxist state can produce the new society that Christianity failed to produce.

The Marxist hope is that the new society will be the end product of the long and gradual transformation from capitalism to communism. As neophyte Christians in Roman times were required to abandon their paganism, so neophyte communists are required to abandon the attitudes and mind-structures acquired by their capitalist upbringing.

In many of his marathon speeches to the Cuban people, Fidel Castro makes frequent reference to those who continue to be captive to the capitalist mentality, to the profit motive. He decries and yet understands the fact that the change from a capitalist mentality to a Marxist mentality is long and tortuous, containing the seeds of sudden reversals. The flight from Cuba which took place after the consolidation of the Cuban Revolution was the flight of seekers-of-profit, the lawyers, dentists, doctors, and businessmen. Only a mere handful of such professionals could adjust to the drastic change involved in serving people instead of exploiting them. The Catholicism of prerevolutionary Cuba did not teach people the nature of injustice; it merely said "Thou shalt not be unjust." The

Cuban Revolution said "Thou shalt not be unjust" and took the logical further step of explaining and exposing injustice. So the Cuban professional class who had never been harassed by their Catholic upbringing in the matter of exploitation now found themselves under the spotlight and under the gun. So, they fled from Havana, moving their base of exploitation to Miami. The entire exploitative mechanism of the Cuban state was blasted from its capitalist moorings by the Castro Revolution, and the exploiters, in total confusion, ran for cover and built new nests in the U.S.A. from which they could continue to prey on the poor, the ignorant, and the sick. The failure of the CIA's attempt to launch a counter-revolution that would result in the overthrow of the Castro government was one of the few "successes" in recent American foreign policy. The forceful restoration of the Cuban capitalist superstructure which might have resulted from a successful CIA invasion would have been a crime against the poor Cuban peasants who had finally achieved dignity and independence.

But capitalism is sick and is gradually dying. This is the hope that we now have at this juncture in history. We are witnessing a deep-rooted and radical change of culture. The economic and cultural base upon which medieval people built Western society is crumbling. Khrushchev, in his famous Pittsburgh speech, was wrong in his timing but he was not wrong when he said that socialism will bury capitalism. The death throes may last another hundred years, but they will most certainly come to an end in one last shuddering gasp. Whether socialism will then become transformed into communism is another question. Communism as a political structure exists today, but communism as a reflection of the teachings of Karl Marx is a very long way off. If it ever does arrive, then Communism, communism, and Marxism will be convertible terms.

6
Communism, the Christian Ideal

The group of believers was one in mind and heart. None said that any of his belongings was his own, but they shared with one another everything they had. . . . There was no one in the group who was in need . . . and the money was distributed to each one according to his need [Acts 4:32, 35].

From each according to his ability and to each according to his need [Karl Marx].

That institutional Christianity has become the gospel turned on its head is nowhere more evident than in the attempt by the institutional Church to discredit communism. Communism, as envisioned by Marx, in its multi-faceted approach to human development, is not a stranger to the gospel of Jesus Christ. It is, at times, a closer reflection of the gospel than is found in the political history of institutional Christianity. Certainly we know that at various times and places the institutional Church has so distorted the original message of the gospel that it became in many ways anti-Christian. I know that this is awfully strong language to use about an institution which is absolutely jam-packed with good intentions, benign rulers, dedicated brothers and sisters, but if we are ever going to understand just how far we can stray from the gospel message and intent then we have to see it as it is. When a Cardinal from New York called the destruction of the Vietnamese people and countryside by the American military machine a crusade to save Western civilization and compared those troops to Christian soldiers in shining armor, then you know that at least that portion of the Church which he represented was not only morally bankrupt but actually decadent. And it is this morally bankrupt and decadent segment of the institutional Church which most vehemently opposes the coming of communism. As a traditional scholastic would argue, if the morally bankrupt and decadent oppose communism then there must be something in communism that is of value.

Early Christians Communistic

The early disciples and apostles interpreted the social content of the gospel message (at least for their time and under their circumstances) as communistic.

> But there was another man, called Ananias. He and his wife, Sapphira, agreed to sell a property; but with his wife's connivance he kept back part of the proceeds, and brought the rest and presented it to the apostles. "Ananias," Peter said, "how can Satan have so possessed you that you should lie to the Holy Spirit and keep back part of the money from the land?" . . . When he heard this Ananias fell down dead. . . . About three hours later his wife came in, not knowing what had taken place . . . Peter said . . . "What made you do it? You hear those footsteps? They have just been to bury your husband; they will carry you out, too." Instantly she dropped dead at his feet [Acts 5:1–9].

I cannot think of any statement in the writings of Karl Marx that gives as dramatic and powerful an expression to the desirability of communism as this New Testament incident. At the very least we must logically argue that communism is not inimical to the gospel message. At most, a socialist enthusiast might argue that it is an ideal to which Jesus beckons us. Apart from the explicit statements in the New Testament, our own intellectual analysis of communism can lead us to the conclusion that communism is a far superior social desideratum than the distribution of wealth which results from the narcissistic and predatory instincts let loose by our predilection for the profit motive. The usurpation of the prophetic role by those who have dedicated a good portion of their energy and talents to the defamation and destruction of communism has not only taken away a Christian option but has at times resembled the obscene excesses of the Inquisition. And just as the Inquisition failed to stop (perhaps abetted) the spread of Protestantism, so it appears that the present stance of the institutional Church shall not prevail against the historical and providential coming of communism (small c).

Exaggerated Egoism

The communal distribution of property is only one of many instances where communism shows itself as the Christian ideal. Another is the studied destruction, both by the early Christians and by Karl Marx, of exaggerated egoism. But the Christian Church had hardly moved beyond the immediate direction and inspiration of Jesus Christ when it fell into the pit of narcissistic egoism. The imperial prerogatives of Constantine slowly interjected themselves into the affairs of the early institutional Church and then later became an integral part of its own fabric and life-style. The glorification of the papacy and the pope was a natural by-product of the intellectual, social, and political trappings of Roman imperialism. The role of Pontiff became the most desired political post in the Western world and the shedding of blood, the hatching of plots, the destruction of opponents and possible challengers, the relegation of matters spiritual to minor clerics, the public persecution and even murder of holy men and women (for example, Joan of Arc) whom God had so evidently raised up in the Church to do his will, all of this was destructive of the main mission of the Church. It was the fertile ground in which developed the institutional Church's acceptance and fierce advocacy of the evil and decadent system of capitalism, and its fierce opposition, in modern times, to communism as a Christian option. Self-glorification and excessive egoism cannot co-exist with the communal implications of communism. "Follow me, for I am meek and humble of heart" would have been a palace joke in the heyday of papal power and self-glorification. We have to say for Karl Marx that he lived and died in abject poverty, in a London tenement. Marx understood that Western culture, aided and abetted by the institutional Church, is a culture fascinated by power and the cult of personality. "Every time I entered the company of men, I returned less a man" (*Imitation of Christ*). Marxist communism is a culture fascinated by the development of a communal, nonegoistic society. Western capitalism is fascinated by the ego. It yearns to attach faces to every fact and statistic, especially if that statistic reflects the making of large amounts of money for doing the inane. Frank Sinatra, Farrah Fawcett-Majors, John Travolta, and Pete Rose are the American folk heroes. This says more about the nature and the state of our culture than volumes of academic research. We have brought rugged individuality to such a degree of insanity that we worship only those whose popular success has raised them far above the crowd and who have become so wealthy that they are enabled (and even expected) to disdain the ordinary and the moral. They become victims of this hero worship and many become so confused by living in their private kingdoms of illusion that they can no longer distinguish between the real and the illusory in their lives. Marilyn Monroe, Howard Hughes, Elvis Presley, and Freddy Prinze are recent victims of the illusions of American (Western)-style hero worship. They became victims of the most insidious form of alienation, self-alienation. They forgot who they were. Their life of illusion became so much a part of their daily living, and their position high above the motley crowd so isolated them, that they became afraid, confused, and increasingly unable to any longer grasp just who it was they were. The canonization of the ego has been one of the most negative results of institutional Christianity. Marxism turns this on its head. The Marxist is not an isolated individual but an essential element in a web of relationships with others. The rugged individual becomes a mere abstraction. As Marx says, man is a being of a species, a communal organism. Any portrayal of the person as a rugged individual is pure rhetoric because such a description does not conform to reality. But it has been an invitation to self-destruction:

> The serpent was the most subtle of all the wild beasts that Yahweh (God) had made. It asked the woman, "Did God really say you were not to eat from any of the trees in the garden?" The woman answered the serpent, "We may not eat it, nor touch it, under the pain of death.". . . Then the serpent said to the wo-

man, "No! You will not die! God knows in fact that on the day you eat it your eyes will be opened and you will be like gods" [Genesis 3:1,5].

Human history is that of the history of the human community. Human transformation lies in the transformation of history.

Communism, The Basis of Religious Life

Of the many ironies and contradictions contained in the institutional Church's condemnation of communism, none is greater than its 2,000-year espousal of communism as the highest expression of religious life. The voluntary sharing of wealth, talents, and social production together with the principle of "from each according to ability and to each according to need" have been the principal pillars of religious life of the Franciscans, the Benedictines, the Dominicans, the Jesuits, Carmelites, Cistercians, and all the other great orders and religious congregations that have sprung up in the Church since Francis, Benedict, Dominic, and Ignatius Loyola. The thought of a modern Dominican or a Jesuit vowed to poverty and the communal life writing fiery tracts against the extension of this same communal life to the population as a whole is ludicrous and a patent self-contradiction. And the fact that Catholic scholars, theologians, institutions of higher learning, conferences of religious superiors, and bishops have not been able to come to an awareness and consciousness of this self-contradiction is only further proof that the human mind has been seriously impaired both by original sin and by the whole illusory religious edifice that has continued to advocate and protect the legacy of Jesus Christ. I am convinced both that the Roman Church is the legitimate heir of Jesus Christ and the only reliable depositor of his message and divinity and that it has distorted and replaced with worldly values and judgments that same message. Communism, not rugged individualism, is the Christian ideal. Communism contradicts and opposes the vices so eloquently described in the gospel message. The rugged individualism of capitalism, so strongly defended by the average cleric, has spawned so much of the vice, murder, egoism, arrogance, and exploitation of the common person (especially in the Third World) that there is no doubt in my mind that if the institutional Church ever came to understand this, have an awareness of this, the huge reservoir of good will and dedication residing there would transform the Church dramatically and return it to its primitive (and accurate) understanding of what the messiahship of Jesus Christ was intended to effect in the world. Communism, not rugged individualism, built the great religious orders when the suppression of personal ego and ambition was accompanied by a channelling of energies and dedication into the dynamics of communal work and worship. Humility produced greatness; suppression of the personal ego in favor of the communal task produced great growth and even a kind of power not originally envisioned by Francis or Dominic. The power let loose by the suppression of the personal ego became so great that a new problem of the collective ego presented itself. It became more important in many cases to be a Dominican or a Jesuit and to identify with the policy of the order than to maintain one's own personal integrity. Here we see the forerunners of the modern "company man." I do not think it an exaggeration to suppose that the reason most of the clergy have little or no social consciousness and in fact stoutly defend the present economic system in spite of its evident decadence is due directly to the fact that to dare raise one's voice is tantamount to being disloyal to the Church or to the order or to one's local bishop. The private and sometimes public denunciation and humiliation of those clergy who do speak out on social issues is deterrence enough. The result is that the communal life (or communism) practiced by the orders, supposedly to free life from material worries in order to allow the unfettered expansion of the spirit, is denied and condemned for the faithful. The institutional Church's active participation both in the defense of capitalism and the condemnation of communism is beginning to be and shall continue to be a millstone tied around its neck.

Marxist and Christian Solidarity

Another area in which radical (original) Christianity and Marxism are reflections of each other is in their emphasis on human solidarity. The real Christian ethic is not the individual moralism often preached by the institution, but rather the profound identification of human beings with their brothers and sisters. This identification is based on our common humanity, the Fatherhood of God, and the fact that "you belong to Christ and Christ belongs to God" (St. Paul; 1 Cor. 3:23). The solidarity expressed in the gospel is a radical message. The best proof that Christians have lost touch with their Christianity is that they fail to be conscious (as were the early Christians) of the radical nature of the message of Christ. Familiarity has bred a dulling of awareness. The New Testament records that many of Jesus's disciples, upon hearing his message "no longer walked with him." So many abandoned him, in fact, that he was prompted to say to the Twelve, "What about you, do you want to go away too?" The doctrine of the incorporation of human beings into the Mystical Body of Christ surpasses in radicalness anything found in Karl

Marx, for it is the most radical and most profound penetration into the heart of the human mystery. The Christian problem is not that the institution lacks doctrine, for with doctrine it has been heavily endowed by the Holy Spirit, but rather that our leadership constantly plays down the radical nature of the message. The message therefore suffers from benign neglect.

It is not as rugged individuals that Christians find salvation in the communion of the Church but as members of that human family which nurtures us at birth and buries us at death. People cannot be islands unto themselves.

After that I saw a huge number, impossible to count, of people from every nation, race, tribe and language; they were standing in front of the throne and in front of the Lamb [Revelation 7: 9].

The liturgical reform movement was a response to the need to rescue the members of the Mystical Body from social and spiritual atomism. The individuals praying all alone in the glow of a soft candle had become the ideal picture of devotion. The Fathers at Vatican II faced the reality that this was typical of the entire withdrawal from the world which the institution had been advocating for far too long a time. The spirituality of the institution had become spiritually-based egoism and self-reflection. It is not so much that this kind of spirituality was wrong as that it was unreal; it failed to take into account the fact that human beings are by nature social. No one can make a case against the doctrine of the Church in this matter, for the Church doctrine has always reflected the communal dimension of human beings. But it did take the action of the bishops at Vatican II to make explicit what had always been implicit in the teachings of the Church. Religion had become an alienation. It is this failing to make explicit what was implicit in the teachings of the Church that caused Marx to engage in a critique of the Church and to declare religion one form of alienation, among others. The Fathers at Vatican II were aware of this:

> Profound and rapid changes make it particularly urgent that no one, ignoring the trend of events or drugged by laziness, content himself with a merely individualistic morality ["The Church in the Modern World," 30].

If Christianity is not a movement of love that creates community, then it is nothing at all. Solidarity with the human race: this is the doctrine of Marxism and of primitive (original) Christianity. What greater sponsorship of human solidarity (in contrast to individualism) could there have been than the historical fact that the Word was made Flesh and dwelt amongst us. Communism (small c) could certainly be advocated on the basis of the Incarnation. That human solidarity, not individualism, was a hallmark of Christianity is evident in the word Ignatius of Antioch used to characterize the meaning and message of the Christian Church, "catholic." This human solidarity advocated both by Marx and by the gospel message is extended to embrace not just the human race, as persons, but also the human race together with its environment. In his letter to the Ephesians Paul describes the plan of God for the world as the recapitulation of all things in Christ. Nothing that is escapes the touch of God through his incarnated Son. All is wrapped up in a unity derived from the creative love and power of God and resanctified and established in unity by the Incarnation. The material is sacred and it is real, not a mere reflection of the human

Communism, the Christian Ideal   69

mind. Any attempt to divide the world into atomistic and mutually antagonistic parts is not from God. This position is clearly taken early in the life of the Christian community by Saint Paul. He states, unequivocally, that the social gap which had existed between the uncircumcised and the circumcised was closed once and for all by the blood of Christ.

> For he is the peace between us . . . and has broken down the barrier which used to keep them apart [Eph. 2:14].

Marx's uncircumcision is transformed into circumcision by Christ, who brought peace and harmony between the two. Christ destroyed the hostility between pagan and Christian. This was to create one single, new person. In his own person he killed the hostility. God willed, through the medium of the Incarnation and Resurrection, the reconstitution of human solidarity once and forever. Marx is the modern prophet who calls us back to human solidarity, but he is not just prophet. He is also the tactician who examines where we are (cultural capitalism) in exhaustive and brilliant analyses and who then beckons us on to where we could be (cultural communism). Human solidarity is his theme. The indwelling of the Trinity, incorporation into Christ, the communion of saints, and the pascal mystery, all cry out for a solidarity of the human race which somehow got lost in the rush of post-Tridentine apologetical theology which accented the juridical and hierarchical. It may at first shock us to think that an "atheist" calls us back to our historical spiritual mission but that is only because we insist on keeping the uncircumcised and circumcised apart, not having either learned or become convinced of Paul's doctrine that Christ had closed the gap and killed the hostility. To kill Marx is to keep the hostility alive. To kill Marx is to make religion into an alienation. Following the rise of the great Catholic philosophers and theologians we became obsessively absorbed in the static analysis of being, dissecting reality into its component and atomistic parts intead of viewing these realities dynamically, as they made their appearance (and disappearance) in the evolving history of humankind. Solidarity implies socialization and socialization is the sign of the times. We must not be jealous or petty or resentful that God chose as his major prophet one not of our own ranks. The actualization of humankind's social dimension, the making of society in terms not of the mythical and abstract but in terms of work and love and affinity to one's neighbor—this is the message of Karl Marx. He reaffirmed in brilliant and prophetic language the place of the human being in the universe. He did not exaggerate, as we learn from Saint Paul:

> We are God's work of art, created in Jesus Christ to live the good life as from the beginning he had meant us to live it [Eph. 2:10].

Socialization is part and parcel of the process of human becoming. It is, of course, the moral dimension of socialization that gives it its primary value, since its historical evolution has perceptibly refined the human conscience vis-à-vis both the local and the world-wide community. The United Nations Organization is a concrete symbol of the communal influence of the growth of socialization, and the sad spectacle of the United States frequently voting in the company of two or three in opposition to the express desires of hundreds of nations of the world speaks

Communism, the Christian Ideal 71

more eloquently than anything else of the poverty of the doctrine of rugged individualism, its moral bankruptcy. The growth of socialization throughout the world has brought about the marvelous communal attitudes of work and neighborliness that we find at the U.N. My experience as a diplomat at the United Nations prompted me to write:

> Nowhere else in the world is there such a total lack of racial or nationalistic tensions, and this is a spiritual event of enormous proportions occurring, significantly, without the assistance of any particular religious institution. . . . What is accomplished naturally in that particular U.N. atmosphere is not happening in the local churches where there is a constant exposure to sermons, parochial school instruction. . . . In the midst of this religious atmosphere, racism flourishes openly, without apology and without resistance from the vast majority of the clergy [*The U.N. Was My Parish* (Denville, N.J.: Dimension Books), p. 17].

The ontological solidarity of which Karl Marx speaks is a universe not of unrelated phenomena but of singular unity in which all of its many parts condition each other reciprocally. "Workers of the world unite." The catholicity of socialization is inherent in Marxist praxis. It reflects a universe whose centerpiece is the human person, a "being of a species." It is in contrast to the atomistic, individualistic thrust of Christianity as we have known it since Constantine. The preoccupation of Christians with the salvation of their own souls induces the very egoism that guarantees their total loss. The social dimension is not a figment of Marxian imagination, but a natural condition arising out of the growing socialization of labor. The great

American ideals of life, liberty, and the pursuit of happiness have meaning only within the context of communal, shared living. The lone, rugged cowboy carries his gun precisely because his enclosed world is often in contrast to and in opposition to the closed world of his neighbor. He survives therefore because he has the power to kill his neighbor. His own economic survival often depends on the economic destruction of the other cowboy. On an international scale we have the absurdity of national leaders declaring that freedom will be maintained because "we have the most powerful arsenal of weaponry in the world." This kind of freedom is the freedom of the jungle. It is a siege-mentality freedom based on egoism. The eschatological community will come into being only when the exaggerated egoism spawned by the inherent demands of the free enterprise system has been overcome by the love spawned by the growing socialization of humanity. The private ownership of the productive facilities of a nation is nothing more than institutionalized egoism, and we must get about the business of replacing it with the communal owership of such facilities. This is a historical and religious imperative. It is the process of liberation and humanization. The institutional Church can play a great role in this historical movement by balancing the Marxist demythologizing of heaven with a disciplined and enlightened demythologizing of the earth.

7
The Diplomat

I shall refer to the diplomat in the masculine gender, but only for convenience. He holds a sensitive position among Eastern bloc diplomats at the United Nations. He is the prototype of those who remain outside the Catholic Church because of the scandalous lack of charity and understanding so prevalent among those whose task it is to bring all things under the saving grace of our Savior. I had seen the diplomat many times in work sessions and in the halls and corridors of the General Assembly, but we had never chatted. I admired him at a distance as he worked tirelessly to coordinate efforts to advance the economic and political interests of the Third World.

I had pointed this out to several Western diplomats, but they did not share my appraisal of the man's intentions. In the cynical atmosphere that pervades politics and diplomacy, he was seen by my colleagues as a man who used his natural enthusiasm and habits of hard work for the sole purpose of expanding his own and his nation's influence. He was credited with being only half-heartedly convinced that an abandonment of capitalist economics could save the poor nations of the world from eternal exploitation. In any case, he was widely admired and respected for his diplomatic skills and was frequently supported by a majority when he introduced resolutions that favored the economic restructuring of the underdeveloped world. However pitiful the state of the world's poor, they can only look with pleading eyes to the affluent West, which induces their poverty by its economic and business policies.

Ironically, if one were to examine the political and religious beliefs of the Christian West, one would expect them to be models of compassion, but in the halls of the United Nations this illusion is quickly shattered. Every Christian nation at the United Nations consistently votes against most of the important measures to promote economic or political development and liberation. The Socialist nations, the "unbelievers," have consistently supported national liberation and freedom for Third World nations. If ever there were people who have eyes but cannot see and have ears but cannot hear, it is those of us who do not recognize that the Christian nations, in their economic and political domination of the poor nations, are a scandal to the world. Not Christianity-as-message but Christianity-as-praxis has been identified with exploitative capitalism.

I took the first available opportunity to make my views known in the Third Committee (the Committee that deals with economic and social affairs). I chided the Western nations for preaching freedom and then practicing it only in that narrow area of the educated and affluent elite. I expressed sympathy with those Western diplomats who knew full well the economic and political implications of the resolutions they were required to introduce and support on behalf of their governments. I did this because I was aware, from private conversations, that many Western diplomats were disgusted with consistently having to support economic exploitation and right-wing dictatorships so that the interests of multinational corporations would be protected. Andrew Young was the first American diplomat in recent history to make some attempt to expose this, but the power of the presidency and the media-educated illiteracy of the American people forced him to retreat. His well-intentioned efforts were in vain. A genuine attempt on the part of the West to tailor its economic policies with a view to developing the economies of the poor nations would signal the end of their own affluence. Evidently, this is something that is not going to happen. It is, therefore, impossible to speak of economic justice in a capitalist society. Capitalism, if it is consistent, generates injustice of its very nature.

> Capitalism has often bred too much misery, too much injustice, too much bitterness and strife. Industrialization itself has not brought these abuses. The wretched system that came along with it has brought evil into being [Paul VI, *The Development of Peoples*, 1967].

My remarks stunned the delegates, not because they had not heard such statements before at the United Nations but rather because, in the words of a delegate from Albania, "a Catholic priest could have said such a thing." The diplomat approached me in the lounge about an hour later. "Father, you sounded like a pre-institutional Christian in your statement this afternoon." He handed me a small book which he had been holding and opened it to a page whose corner had been turned down and pointed out a passage from the first page of Friedrich Engels' *The Book of Revelation*. "Read here," he said, as he pointed out the third paragraph:

> One good thing, however, Ernest Renan has said: "When you want to get a distinct idea of what the

first Christian communities were, do not compare them to the parish congregations of our day; they were rather like local sections of the International Working Men's Association. Christianity, like every great revolutionary movement, was made by the masses."

We sat beneath the huge painting of the Great Wall, a gift to the United Nations from the People's Republic of China, and settled in for a long chat. For refreshment, I had an orange drink and he ordered two large glasses of tomato juice. Before I had a chance to comment on the passage he had asked me to read, he began to speak about his family and how he missed his children; he spoke about a visit to Harlem which he and an aide had made just a few days before. He talked about President Kennedy and how his eyes had filled with tears when he heard of his death. He remarked that just as in the United States people would always recall where they were and what they were doing when the news of Kennedy's assassination broke, so the same thing was true in his native land. Many of his relatives, who had long ago abandoned going to Church, went immediately to the nearest church and "meditated." He volunteered that he had been baptized a Catholic and that as a youth he had been captivated by the liturgy. It supplied a warmth and an other-worldliness which was in sharp contrast to the bitter poverty of his family and his neighbors. "In this sense," he said, "Marx was absolutely right when he called religion the opiate of the people." I agreed with him even though I hedged my answer by emphasizing that this need not necessarily be the case; that for the educated religious person religion need not be an opiate at all. I suggested that a mass meeting in Peking to extol the virtues of Mao Zedong could be used as an opiate even though Mao did in fact

The Diplomat 77

make a great contribution to Chinese development and history. He obliged by agreeing.

We then gradually moved to a discussion on various matters pending before the General Assembly. He suggested that perhaps I could caucus informally with him and his group on matters on which we had a common stand. I welcomed the idea and we immediately went into several matters before the Committees at that time, the question of the United Nations presence in Korea, the question of the violation of civil rights in Chile, and political developments in Belize. We then went right from the lounge to a committee room where we discussed these matters with others of his group and one man from our own diplomatic mission. It turned out to be my first lesson in how back-room politics worked at the United Nations.

I was to see quite a bit of my friend the diplomat in the weeks and months to come. On almost every important issue affecting the interests of the Third World nations we would meet informally in the delegates' lounge or sometimes in a little restaurant directly across the street from the Secretariat entrance to the United Nations. It was there that I introduced him to the delights of Italian cuisine. He soon became a devotee of a wide range of pastas and, of course, veal parmigiana, a specialty of that particular restaurant. From the first, I was conscious of the fact that our meetings would have to be discreet, since East European delegates are subject to more than the ordinary amount of surveillance. Not that there was anything to hide, since neither of us was trying to "convince" the other of anything.

We both had something to gain by these meetings. He was fascinated with the clerical mind that could agree with him that socialism had a value. I, for my part, learned a lot about the inner workings of the United Nations and its various departments. Just as in any other organization, there are right ways and wrong ways to present one's case, and there are channels through which one has a better chance of succeeding in the adoption of a particular resolution. One must learn the politics of the place. I also acquired many insights into the policies, aims, and strategies of East European diplomats. My friend the diplomat at no time ever revealed anything to me that one could consider "secret." He was, in every way, a loyal and dedicated public servant, who passionately believed in Marxist socialism. But, in three years of hundreds of discussions on every subject from the role of the Palestinian Liberation Organization, to the Russian and Chinese meanings of democracy, I became familiar with the Socialist approach to world issues. Of one thing I became certain, the Socialist world is a more idealistic and honest world in its desire to be a force for good than is the West. Western diplomats do not even pretend idealism in actual negotiations. Economic expansion is almost always the basis for diplomatic initiatives. The control of raw materials, the protection of capital investments around the globe, the guarantee of a continued military presence in some strategic part of the world: these are the top priorities of Western diplomatic discussions.

Just how strongly old-timers feel about such issues is well illustrated by the attitude of the director of a CCD program for a parish outside Washington, D.C. He is a former CIA officer who had been assigned to Saigon. He approached me one afternoon in a state of great agitation. "I am seriously considering early retirement, Father, after what I was told today down at headquarters. They have taken away our authority to assassinate." Of course, James Bond exists in Eastern Europe also and the same brutal, nihilistic methods are common there as well. The fact that such policies consistently fail to attain their ends is absolutely no deterrent to their continued use. One would think that the tragedy of Vietnam, if from no other perspective than that of our having lost to a mini-army, would be reason enough to at least question the usefulness of such methods. But the demand for more of the same goes on and even gets stronger after every defeat. It is sheer madness, and this madness is very often defended in the most righteous terms.

It surely is not in this area of foreign policy that the Socialist nations seem to be more honest and helpful to the Third World, but rather in the area of economic assistance. From my own personal experience I have learned that many arrangements made with Third World nations on the level of economic assistance truly are designed to lead to eventual self-sustaining growth. Western economic assistance, on the other hand, is always closely tied in with a further expansion of the economic power of the multinational corporations. Such assistance, furthermore, takes place within existing world market frameworks, even though it is these very market frameworks that cause underdevelopment in the first place and frustrate every attempt at development and every attempt to create self-sustaining economic growth. The logic of optimum profits is entirely incompatible with the needs and aspirations of the underdeveloped world and yet there is not one international aid organization in the West that is predicated on any other philosophy. In short, Western society, for all its rhetoric, has no intention of bringing about self-sustaining economic growth in any underdeveloped nation. In fact, behind the facade of piety and democracy, its intention is to do the exact opposite. Self-sustaining growth means progressive economic independence and progressive economic independence is precisely what the multinational corporation (and the government under which it flies its flag) will fight to the death. And it will use any arm of (for example) the American government, such as the Central Intelligence Agency, to see to it that underdevelopment remains a permanent condition throughout the nonindustrialized world.

For all of America's talk about aid to underdeveloped countries, the fact is that only one-fifth of one percent of our GNP goes to foreign aid. And even this insignificant portion of our wealth is not given away without strings attached. Much of the money given as "aid" comes right back to the United States in the form of salaried Americans working in the recipient nation and in the form of purchases of American goods. Foreign aid is often no more than the subsidization of American technicians and American companies. As Kenneth Galbraith put it:

> Though we have much and the remainder of the world is poor, we are singlemindedly devoted to getting more [*The Affluent Society* (Boston: Houghton Mifflin, 1971), p. 104].

In their excellent book, *The Myth of Aid*, Denis Goulet and Michael Hudson observe:

> The anti-developmental aspects of their preferred neo-classical and Malthusian doctrines are seen to reflect the aid-lenders' preference for technological palliatives and population control as alternatives to social and economic modernization in the aid-borrowing countries [New York: IDOC, 1971, p. 75].

The pious protestations of Western lenders and the lack of such piety on the part of Socialist lenders reminds me of the biblical story where the son who said he would go out and work in the vineyard did not, while the one who said

The Diplomat 81

he would not, did. Jesus' comment on this situation was: "I tell you solemnly even the tax collectors and prostitutes are making their way into heaven before you" (the one who said he would but did not). There is absolutely no doubt in my mind that the "atheistic" diplomat who does (however unconsciously) the will of the Father will be heartily welcomed into the kingdom of heaven and that the Christian diplomat who does not won't make it at all.

The moral implications of all these matters which came before the United Nations was a source of many conversations with my diplomat friend in the lounge. And then, one Friday afternoon he approached me at that little room downstairs in the General Assembly where delegates pick up the documents set aside for their particular diplomatic mission. "What about a ride up to Connecticut tomorrow morning early. We'll get to see all the foliage and there are a few things I would like to talk over with you." He knew that I had many friends in Connecticut and that I could make arrangements to have the privacy of a guest cottage for our discussions. "I'll pick you up in Brooklyn, at 8 A.M. sharp," he said. The next morning, right on time, the diplomat pulled up in front of Saint Gregory the Great parish rectory, in one of his diplomatic mission's limousines. His personal car, he apologized, was in a garage with a stalling problem. It was a beautiful October day and the diplomat was to see all the October color he had hoped for, and more. As we crossed the Whitestone Bridge, the view of a church spire reminded me that Notre Dame was playing football that afternoon, so I asked my friend if he would agree to interrupt our talk during the game and enjoy the game with me. He agreed and even suggested that I teach him the rules of the game as we watched. He later became a great fan of Notre Dame and never missed a game if he was in the country. When Notre Dame won the national championship in 1977, I received a cable from Paris, where the diplomat was engaged in discussions. It read: "Our Lady did it again."

The ride up to Fairfield County did not take as long as it should have. The possession of DPL plates and diplomatic immunity is a temptation to speed that my diplomat friend did not resist. But even the high speed could not blur the beauty of the countryside and my friend remarked that he was a great admirer of rural America. He observed that the affluence of Westchester and Fairfield counties could not be duplicated anywhere else in the world and that America was singularly capable of extending such affluence to a much larger segment of the population. He wondered how a mixed population of peoples from all over the world could find the kind of unity required to produce such technological excellence and such productivity. He conceded that the freedom to do economic evil also allowed for the blossoming of all sorts of talents and ingenuity on the part of the American people. It was obvious that what the world needed was a proper balance between political and economic freedom and the need to protect the not so talented in the society from exploitation, to see that the sick and the aged had security regardless of their ability to produce. Every Communist government, on its way to power, experienced the tenacity and even ferocity of the privileged classes. Christian peoples have always fought to the bitter end to retain their right to exploit their neighbor.

It was this phenomenon that led Marx to come to the conclusion that a dictatorship of the proletariat was an absolute, if regrettable, necessity. Revolution, he observed, is the by-product of the refusal of the monied classes to compromise, even one iota, their power to exploit their fellow citizens. Revolution is nothing more than the physical expression of inward rage. It does not, of

The Diplomat

itself, bring political freedom and economic justice. What nation, what ideology, what revolution would finally accomplish this great human objective? Many forms of government would fall and much needless suffering would take place before this problem would be resolved.

We stopped in Port Chester for coffee and apple pie. The diplomat wondered why his compatriots had never made apple pie. He called it one of America's greatest inventions. A small crowd of teenagers greeted us as we emerged from the diner. They were admiring the large limousine and wondered if the President or some other government official was in town. My friend introduced himself and we spent about 10 minutes as he fielded questions from these youngsters. Surprisingly, he got not one question about communism or capitalism or even about the United Nations. They asked about dress and food and customs of his native land. If only adults could relate to other adults of different religious or ideological persuasions with this same naturalness and simplicity. There would then be no deep and permanent confrontations. Their friendliness warmed him considerably and we idealized about a possible happy world in the future when adults could be as nice as kids. This was our theme as we continued our journey into Connecticut.

We passed through a long circular driveway framed by columns of white birch and pulled up in front of a large white colonial. Our host was waiting to greet us. He was a man of great learning and a highly developed sense of confidentiality, a virtue that made him a precious host for a number of diplomatic meetings I arranged at his estate. His own natural humility and reserve soon dissipated any fear of exposure on the part of participants. They sought and got a private place free from the curiosity of the press and fellow diplomats. The "cottage" was actually a completely self-contained house with two bedrooms, two baths, and all the amenities and conveniences of a suburban home.

After our host had departed my diplomat friend got right to the point. He had a firm conviction, he said, that the economic analysis of capitalism begun by Marx and developed as changes took place both socially and in the marketplace, is the basis for the transformation of society from a condition of injustice to a condition of justice. But he had also observed in Eastern Europe over the past twenty years that the attempt to create this condition of justice and economic equality in a nonreligious atmosphere is unnatural and deprives the people, to the extent that it succeeds, of that fullness of personality which only the worship of God develops. In succeeding, therefore, it fails. He had observed in the highest councils of Marxist governments an almost tangible tension, an unspoken need to include that which was always studiously excluded. My friend then caught me by surprise and said: "If the Catholic Church ever comes to terms with the need to jettison its obscene attachment to unbridled capitalism and matures enough to escape from its self-imposed ignorance of the high moral condition and dignity of hundreds of millions of peoples who have chosen the Socialist path, it would unleash a thunder of spirituality throughout Eastern Europe that would create for the first time in history, the Christian community." The diplomat uttered these words with such unaccustomed emotion that I was completely taken aback and sat in stunned silence for several minutes.

"We Marxists," he continued, "have created for humankind the economic framework for a condition of peace and justice. It is now up to the Catholic Church to infuse this structure with a soul. This is its historical mission and its continued refusal to do this constitutes its major sin, its mortal sin. You and I, Father, must work toward that end with all our energy and all our mind." These words, coming from a dedicated and highly placed Marxist left me almost speechless as I groped for something to say. He filled the lull in the conversation by asking what potential there was now existing within the institution for a progressive change of attitude. I outlined for him as best I could the various theological and social trends within the Church structure that lent hope that the issue of economic justice would one day become a dominant one in the Catholic Church. I explained to him the meaning and general content of liberation theology. At the cottage I always kept a small selection of economic and theological works for use when I visited there. We read together Paul VI's *Development of Peoples*. The similarity between the prophetic language of Karl Marx and the passionate defense of economic justice found in this encyclical was too clear to go without observation and discussion. We then spent a good deal of time reading and commenting on John XXIII's concept of socialization. This was not an easy task but it was worthwhile and in that concept, perhaps, lies the soul that can infuse the cold economic structure of Marxist economic theory.

Unfortunately, the theological disciplines are not sufficiently familiar with the laws of economics to be of much use as yet to the development of John's concept of socialization. The theologians need a good deal of time to inform themselves of the language and history of economic theory before a well-developed theology of liberation and economic justice will be produced in the Church. Of course, before a well-informed group of theologians emerge it would first be necessary to modify, perhaps rather drastically, the kind of academic preparation given to seminarians. So, it would be unrealistic to expect any progress for a very long time, at least in that direction. Perhaps events in Third World countries will bring about, among Christians, a grassroots appreciation for the need for reform in matters economic. The whole thing may take place in the streets.

The diplomat found Pope John's concepts acceptable to Marxists but, since it has not as yet been accepted by even one Christian nation, it leaves the Church's advocacy of social justice in the realm of theory. The potential, however, is enormous, for John's theology reflects modern preoccupation with the future, as terrestial, as operative, in contrast to a contemplative understanding of the world and humankind's role in it. The diplomat and I agreed that John XXIII's and the Marxian view of humankind's historical march into the future are only semantically different. John takes as an operative assumption that the socialization of society has already taken place and is now in the process of shedding archaic antisocialistic societal forms. He did not want the Church to be riding the crest of a wave of individualism moving against a surging sea of socialization, however majestic and ascetic it may appear in its splendid isolation. The secularization of society, proclaimed by Marx as the future, is recognized by Pope John as the present.

That this humble, joyous man, no doubt inspired by the Holy Spirit, possessed an insight not necessarily shared by the hierarchy as a whole, is evidenced by the fact that many pastoral statements completely ignore and in some cases directly contradict this giant of the papacy. It was the diplomat's conviction that if the Christians were to find a body politic in which the social doctrine of John and Paul could become incarnate, the Communist-Catholic cold war would dissipate like snow cast into a blazing furnace. He believed that hundreds of millions of Marxists hungered for the brotherly love that only the Fatherhood of a Living God can produce and that if the "real" Christianity ever emerged all humankind would call itself Christian. The attraction of the gospel being lived would be irresistible. The closed cosmos of the Greek world would once again revert to the open-ended historical world of the Hebrew, a world of a humanity in close touch with the Living God. The use of the human intelligence could then emerge from the closet in which it has been held captive by the people who burned Joan of Arc at the stake and condemned Galileo. Heaven and earth would meet and kiss in unfettered, demythologized faith. The Marxists have succeeded in capturing the imagination of over half the world's population because they have avoided the mistake of modern theology, the re-presentation of the gospel message as re-presentation of the past. Such an interpretation freezes humanity in an unnatural religious and socio-economic environment precisely because it is not oriented toward the future, but looks always to a dead past. If this historical institutional pattern can be broken, the world would belong to Christ, the Christ for whom it now groans in anticipation. The diplomat revealed himself as a man of deep faith in this moment of the dramatic unfolding of his inner self.

This meeting was the first of several trips to the Connecticut countryside. It became increasingly obvious to me that my diplomat friend was a deeply religious man. And it was precisely here that he suffered his greatest pain. I am sure that he wanted to express his religious faith in union with a congregation of believers praising God, but feared an immediate dilution of its content if shared within the context of the institutional Church, which appears wedded to and publicly defends an economic system which is the source of so many of the evils and so much of the corruption and suffering in the world today. To find a way out of this dilemma was his greatest desire and he continued to hope that somewhere in the many discussions we had been having he might find a personal answer. He never did.

Since the General Assembly meetings at the United Nations begin on the third Tuesday of September, our personal discussions in Connnecticut came at a time when we were also both very busy in our committee work. Added to this, the diplomat had to make a trip back to Eastern Europe for consultations with his government on several matters concerning the General Assembly agenda, so we broke off our meetings temporarily. His influence at the United Nations continued to remain strong as he was a leader in the composition of many resolutions which appealed to the imagination of the delegates and which often aided in the settling of many thorny issues. He is a master of intelligent compromise.

At the International Conference on the Law of the Sea, which was to take place a year after I had begun to talk with him, he fired the imagination of the U.N. delegates when he called for rejection of the geopolitical regionalism of the nineteenth century, based on sovereignty, ownership, and power and a movement toward a sea-oriented regionalism founded on the concept of cooperation, the common heritage of humankind, and the transformation of the concept of sovereignty along with that of ownership. He made a strong argument that as part of a new international order an overlapping of different social systems would increase social stability and reduce conflict. He called for the various existing regional intergovernmental organizations, such as EEC, COMECON, and OAS to have a special relationship with a central Seabed Authority. Energizing him all the time was a secular version of the prayer of Christ that "all may be one, Father, as you and I are one." His daily actions were religious but packaged in the secularism of Marxist terminology. This Marxist diplomat wants to see all the brothers and sisters of this world at peace and working for common goals. It is regrettable that the energy used by the institutional Church in combating the earlier heresies is now dissipated in a meaningless struggle against atheistic Marxism; meaningless because a quiet and understanding dialogue between the two "religions" could only conclude with the surprising fact that the atheist has come a long way and has laid the basis for a Christianity that is about to come of age. An understanding of this by the institutional Church would dramatically transform the world. It is a day for which my Marxist friend and I continually pray.

During a rather long and sometimes boring debate in the Security Council just before Thanksgiving Day of that year, the diplomat slipped me a Happy Thanksgiving Day card, a large turkey cutting up a smaller turkey for dinner. Inside the card he had written: "The problem, Father Pat, is this, how the Lamb of the institutional Church can lie down with the lion of Marxism." How true. This indeed has become an historical necessity and becomes more and more evident as we see that, unlike many of the historical "isms" which conflicted with the Church in the past, this "ism" shows no sign of abating. On the contrary, it has gripped the imagination of the world and appears to be here to stay. A new economic force has entered history and it has strong moral overtones and implications, since it declares the economic model of the Christian nations to be evil. In its atheism it hurls thunderbolts of eternal damnation on those who willfully and knowingly practice, defend, abet, and justify the capitalist economic way of life. It has infuriated the righteous element of the institution, for it has struck them at the very marrow of their piety. And perhaps they foresee, through the cloudy veil of their indignation, that Khrushchev was right when he said in Pittsburgh that Marxism will bury capitalism.

Perhaps the prophetic Marx embraced the lost eschatology of the early Christian vision. It appears that as humiliating as it may be for some elements in the institution, the future-look of socialism will either have to be embraced or imitated. There is no way out because history is moving and marching straight in that direction. It is inevitable that Marxism and Catholicism will come to an historic understanding, because *ecclesia est universale sacramentum spei pro* totius *mundi salute* (the Church is the universal sacrament of hope for the good of the *entire* world). Those elements in the institution who wish it to remain a private club of those who pray in a particular way will ultimately be defeated by the workings of the Holy Spirit in history. Socialism has become a necessary thing in a time of a quickly decaying Christian culture. The evil of the profit motive, the basis for capitalism, has eroded and seriously tainted the integrity of the institution itself. The Message will always remain as it is, but the form of the society in which it is preached will change. It must change if the Church is to fulfill its mission to call all to the saving power of Christ. I believe that Peter will one day stand up before the assembly of the people of God and will address himself to those members of the Mystical Body who are now far away and he will address them in the loving and pastoral words of Saint Paul:

> Bear in mind that you were at that time without Christ, excluded as aliens from the community of Israel, and strangers to the covenants of the promise; having no hope, and without God in the world. But now in Christ Jesus you, who were once afar off, have been brought near through the blood of Christ [Eph. 2:12].

The Diplomat

The signs of the times are that this Body of Christ, this bark of Peter, cannot much longer listen to those voices of hate and suspicion, of narrowness and ignorance, for Christ is the Savior of every Marxist and his victory must be complete. The love of Christ for millions of Chinese and Russians and Vietnamese is soon to burst through the walls of prejudice. The historical transformation of humankind is not far off. The Old Testament belief in the promises of the Living God demands an eschatological theology, and if the theologians deny us such a theology, then the Holy Spirit will produce it from the hearts and souls of the people in the streets.

The diplomat sent me a Christmas card from Eastern Europe. The General Assembly had completed its business in early December and many of the delegates headed home for the holidays. The diplomat was due to return to New York in mid-January with a stopover in Geneva on government business. His Christmas card was traditional with the Virgin, Child, and St. Joseph surrounded by shivering animals in the stable at Bethlehem. In his own hand he added,

Christus vincit, Christus regnat, Christus imperat

The card was sent to the rectory in Brooklyn. It came two days before Christmas, so I placed it on my desk and meditated on its meaning during the Christmas days. I took it as a signal that this holy season had brought about an additional grace in the soul of my Marxist friend. Christmas Eve I heard confessions for two hours, from 6 to 8 P.M., in the dimly-lit Church of Saint Gregory the Great, on Brooklyn Avenue. The glitter of vigil lights, green, red, blue, and white never seemed so beautiful or meaningful.

The Church was quiet and I prayed for the diplomat. He was alone with his thoughts about his Savior, in an atmosphere dedicated to silence on that subject. And even if that were not so he would not dare to speak, lest his mind and heart be torn asunder and he and his children become vulnerable to an opiate so overwhelmingly sweet and desirable that even the withdrawal of freedom and dignity would proceed unnoticed. How his heart must have yearned to kneel in front of a simple crib and cry out from the depth of his soul, silent night, holy night! Like Simone Weil he could not allow himself this sweetness until the institutional Church purifies itself of its almost neurotic attachment to the past. The diplomat also belongs to a Church of silence. And in this Church there are not the consolations of martyrdom.

8
A Tribute to Jamal Baroody

Baroody is the most conspicuous figure in the United Nations, and it pays to ask oneself why [William Buckley, Jr.].

A small notice in the Detroit *Free Press* caught my eye. Jamal Baroody, Saudi Arabia's Ambassador to the United Nations, was dead. My first reaction was one of shock. No matter how reasonable it is that a friend who is getting old may one day simply fall down and die, the news is always startling. My second reaction was one of annoyance. Jamal Baroody was "Mr. United Nations" to all of his fellow delegates, the oldest in years of service (from day one) and the most dramatic speaker and brilliant analyst of the thousands of delegates who come and go over the years. He was the only delegate at the United Nations to receive (on several occasions) enthusiastic rounds of applause from his confreres. But the Detroit *Free Press* barely acknowledged his passing away. I doubt if he did much better in the rest of the press across the country.

It is characteristic of the American press that it is unconscionably ignorant of U.N. matters and personalities and extremely slanted in its view of the policies adopted by the majority of its members. At times, the New York press was more than ignorant, it was intimidated. I was once asked by a senior editor of the *Amsterdam News*, the New York City black newspaper, to write a series of articles on the Palestinian question. This same editor called me about a week later to tell me that at a meeting at the paper's office in Manhattan it was decided not to go ahead with the articles for fear of violence from the Jewish Defense League. A measure of the American press's lack of appreciation and understanding of United Nations matters and also its fear of intimidation from strong lobbying groups was its lionizing of the boorish and downright insulting behavior of Daniel Moynihan when he was our Ambassador to the United Nations. I suppose it is simply another reflection of our immaturity in foreign affairs that so arrogant and diplomatically incompetent a delegate should be highly praised while an extremely competent and sensitive diplomat like Jamal Baroody gets a few lines on a back page.

Baroody's wit, penetrating intellect, compassion, and outrageous humor made him a superstar among the delegates. "He derails trains of thought, discomfits the orthodox, and disrupts debate" (*Time*). On many occasions fellow delegates would run up to each other and shout: "Baroody is speaking in the General Assembly," and we would all rush in to be informed and entertained. Some delegates pretended to be bored by Baroody's long speeches, but even they could not resist listening. He was brilliant and charismatic. He advised and scolded delegates about their voting records, their attitudes toward religion, racism, and politics. He chided Americans for being too arrogant and threatened to punish the Russians if their appetite for power got out of hand. During the debate between the Soviet Union and China, a Russian

A Tribute to Jamal Baroody 95

diplomat observed: "The oratorical skill of the distinguished delegate is almost overpowering. He was like a god."

The long corridor that contains the Security Council and the Council for Economic and Social Affairs is lined on one side by a good number of elegant lounge chairs; the other side contains one simple, very uncomfortable bench, located near the rest room. Baroody liked to sit there and it was there that we had most of our chats. I believe he sat on that uncomfortable bench because of his desire (perhaps fantasy would be a better word) of living the life of an ascetic. He once told me: "I wish I had the leisure to live the life of an ascetic. But how is that possible when we diplomats have to entertain and travel on government business. The U.N. should be located on monastery grounds. You must speak to your Cardinal about that. Only ascetics make sound judgments."

Baroody's fiery and electrifying speeches were followed immediately by a contrasting calm and repose. His speech finished, he would, Groucho Marx-like, shuffle from delegate desk to delegate desk, sharing a simple and delightful banter with his colleagues. To a woman delegate from Tanzania, a friend of mine, he once said: "Don't tell my fellow Arab chauvinists I said this, but you women delegates from Tanzania are among the best this United Nations has ever produced." He did not mind exaggerating a bit if he thought it would buoy up someone's spirits. I got close to Baroody because he shared my distaste for capitalism and my frustration that, as Christians, we could not attack the system without being labeled as anti-Christian, or antidemocratic, or pro-Communist.

My first encounter with this great man took place shortly after I had arrived at the United Nations. The occasion was the day I made my first statement during a debate in the Third Committee. The statement was a brief one, but it either stunned, shocked, or pleased my fellow delegates. I said (in part):

> I feel sorry for those delegates who represent the developed capitalist member-states. They are fully aware that it is the nature of capitalism to thrive on exploitation. And yet, these delegates, loyal citizens of their respective countries, are required to defend and even promote these very policies of exploitation. I feel compassion for them because so many of them are good men. It's like the man who is a nice guy but gets a job as a used-car salesman.

These words, which I considered unexceptional, had the delegates in consternation. A Catholic priest, apparantly, was never expected to talk like this. One delegate was so unbelieving that he approached me afterwards and said he would not be satisfied that I was serious unless I personally told him I was not being sarcastic, or just simply joking. The delegate from Albania asked for a copy of the statement. Baroody met me downstairs in the General Assembly building near the coat racks. "May I invite you up to the lounge for a drink, Father," he said as he extended his hand in friendship. How could I resist an invitation from such a marvelous personality. I put my coat back in the rack and accompanied Baroody upstairs. As we rode the escalator back to the main hall of the General Assembly a member of the Irish delegation passed us on the down escalator. She stared at me with a furious expression on her face. She must have wondered how this terrible priest could have insulted all of Western Christian civilization!

In my years at the U.N., the Irish delegation studiously avoided me and would sit fuming as I delivered one

A Tribute to Jamal Baroody 97

"heretical" speech after another. Baroody observed the woman's anger and whispered to me as she passed, "She'll report you to the little priest from the Vatican." "The little priest" was the Holy See's observer in the Third Committee, who had the reputation for extremely right-wing views and a permanently sour facial expression. I know that this will seem like a gross exaggeraton, but I never saw him smile. The poor man was constantly horrified and terrified at what he heard at the United Nations and could never understand why I voted with the U.N. majority in criticizing the Chilean junta. He spent so much time trying to get me to make statements in favor of the junta (he himself, as an observer, could not) that I became convinced (incorrectly) that he must be a Chilean citizen. I myself was amazed that a priest would be so strongly in favor of a brutal regime that has been condemned all over the world, in hundreds of forums. I showed him copies of statements made by members of the Chilean hierarchy, complaining about the violation of civil rights in Chile. His response was always brief and to the point. "The generals are anti-Communist." After some attempts at dialogue with the man, I finally took to simply avoiding him. Fortunately for the Holy See, he did not reflect his mission's attitude, which was far more enlightened and humane.

Baroody and I discussed the nature of capitalism. From his vantage point at the United Nations he had observed for many years its devastating effects on Third World nations, who were used as pawns in the struggle among superpowers for more and more control over the world's resources. He spoke up whenever he saw the contest of greed get too intense. Commenting on the uselessness of such struggles for power, he once said: "The wind and the sea had a quarrel, but the one who paid the price was the sailor in the boat. We are all of us in the boat." He was philosophic about the possibility of a change in the order of things. He often said: "The people who suffer the most by the system are kept in such ignorance of how it works that they often become its strongest defenders. Like Nixon's silent majority."

There was a strongly religious side to Baroody. An Arab Christian who represented the most orthodox Muslim country in the world, he spoke lovingly of the Blessed Virgin, while warning religious people that they could be offensively hypocritical. Baroody was fascinated by religion and he never ceased to defend and illustrate his arguments with quotations from Holy Scipture. One day I gave him a rosary that had been blessed by Pope Paul VI, and until the day I left New York and the U.N. he never ceased to thank me for it. "I am going to use this rosary of the Church against the Church" he told me one day. "I am going to pray that the Catholic Church will one day come to an understanding of the moral aspects of economics. The question of capitalism is a religious question, but unfortunately religious people do not want to touch it." I pointed out that good Pope John and the intense Paul VI had given a lot of attention to the subject, but I did concede that it does not seem to have caused much of a ripple in the Church. Baroody was a survivor and he was careful how he phrased his public statements on the relationships between religion and economic justice. After all, he was the Ambassador from Saudi Arabia and it is the sheiks that run the show there. He was always the diplomat. I was once able to observe his diplomatic expertise in a matter directly involving my job as economic advisor to the Prime Minister of Grenada.

It was a very cold and blustery December afternoon when I was called to the Prime Minister's suite at the Waldorf Towers. The secretary at the Grenada Mission told me that the matter was urgent and I was to get over

A Tribute to Jamal Baroody 99

there as quickly as I could. The Secret Service men knew me, so I was ushered right into the Prime Minister's suite. To my great surprise Jamal Baroody was sitting there chatting with the Prime Minister. My surprise was due to the fact that a member of our mission had long ago convinced the Prime Minister that he should not have anything to do with the Arabs, since the Israelis could do serious damage to the tourist trade in Grenada. I had been urging the Prime Minister in the opposite direction. I had asked him on many occasions to reconsider his position, not only because I saw it as a dead-end policy for the long term but also because the Palestinian cause was so just and so prominent a part of the U.N. discussions that the Arabs would remember those who were consistent supporters of the Israeli cause when things changed.

The member of our mission who was so strongly against any ties with the Arabs greeted me effusively as I entered the room. In a flash I figured out the whole scenario. The Prime Minister had decided to play it both ways. The Arabs had the money. I wanted to warn Baroody that he was being led into a trap, but it was impossible. There were too many people milling around. Obviously, my friendship with Baroody was the reason I was sent for, and no doubt I was sent for after all had already gathered because the Prime Minister knew that I would have strongly questioned what was going on if I had been brought in on the matter earlier. The Prime Minister turned to me and said, "Father Pat, I was just telling Ambassador Baroody how pleased I was that you had given him a rosary blessed by the pope. I was telling him also how pleased I have always been that you and he are good friends." The stuff was getting high enough to shovel out. Then Gairy went on to say how pleased his government would be to support the just Arab causes if only he were given enough money so as not to have to worry about an Israeli-inspired embargo of Grenada tourism. He wanted ten million right away and more to be negotiated later.

Baroody handled the entire affair beautifully. He smiled all around, with folded arms, as he watched them try to trap him. He led them on, nodding affirmatively and saying, "Ah, yes," "Oh, indeed." Having made their case and convinced that they had Baroody just where they wanted him, they stopped and waited with baited breath for his reply. Millions of dollars hung in the balance. Baroody enjoyed the drama and added to it by coughing repeatedly during the silence and then sending a waiter off to another room to bring him a coke. He handed the coke to me and asked me if I would please pour it for him and he winked a devilish wink, as he did so. I knew Baroody had everything under control. "Isn't it a shame," he said very slowly and looking only at me, "that the modern world has made borrowing a few dollars so complicated. But I do wish the Prime Minister a nice visit in New York." And then, turning to Gairy, he said: "Unfortunately, all requests for aid must go through the Arab League. But I do look forward to meeting you again the next time you are in New York." With that, he stood up, shook my hand, and walked straight out of the suite without another word. I could not wait to see Baroody alone and I got my opportunity the next day in the Security Council gallery. "You certainly handled yourself well, yesterday," I remarked. Baroody just smiled and said, "I am surrounded by avarice all the time and while I don't like it, I've learned to handle it." Baroody saw the handwriting on the wall for colonialism and capitalism but he knew how to wait and he knew that he himself would never experience the just society in his beloved Saudi Arabia in his lifetime, but he never ceased to lay a foundation for it. Bill Buckley said, "Baroody is the most conspicuous figure in the United

Nations, and it pays to ask oneself why." Just remember what Baroody stood for, Mr. Buckley, and you will have your answer.

9
The Decline of a Marxist

It was a lovely summer afternoon, and I was staying at the home of Vivian Cuppage, in Wimbledon, England. Vivian's large Georgian home is around the corner from the Wimbledon Tennis Courts, in the nicest suburb of London. The Wimbledon games were in progress. I could have had a ticket but preferred to have a TV set out in the middle of a spacious, sumptuously green lawn that blanketed a large area of land behind Vivian's house. One of Vivian's sons was a budding TV producer, and he knew what wires and antennae to put where and produced a perfect picture. I don't know what the secret of British television is, but you never get sickly greens, reds, and purples on British television.

Chris Evert was well on her way to winning her second Wimbledon championship in a row. Her opponent was a young British woman who simply could not match the skilled intensity of the American. I took a special pride in her success, because the British view of Americans is that they have neither the self-discipline nor the dedication to produce excellence. That this myth has been exploded many times over, somehow does not seem to lessen its hold on the British public, even though it can get very excited about American personalities. There may be a bit of subconscious resentment at seeing what was their colony succeed them in the leadership of world affairs. That day in Wimbledon held another excitement for me. I was going to meet that very evening with a man I had admired from a distance for years, Cheddi Jagan, former Prime Minister of Guyana, in South America. He is one of those men, too good to be true, an innocent in the jungle of national and international politics. I often thought of him as a Mr. Magoo, unaware of the dangers passing all around him. His integrity, openness, charity, and fundamental humility are enveloped in a charm and gentleness that are almost bewitching. In one of his early political campaigns, moved by the sorry plight of blacks and Indians in the colonial situation, he shouted, "We shall turn the guns on those oppressors who now turn them on us." But when the opportunity came, he couldn't do it. Like his mentor, Marx, he was seized with the passion, the oratory, and explosiveness of the prophet. His soul cried out for the redress of ancient injustices.

He was one of those, like Marx, whose fire was ignited from above. These prophets feel, see, experience, and comprehend what often entirely escapes the notice of their contemporaries. And so they appear to be radical, sometimes evil and frightening. And the irony is that these people, these radicals, are usually so gentle, so easily moved to compassion, so beautiful in the eyes of their God, who has chosen them to be his disciples and prophets, to reach out to the poor and the oppressed on his behalf. And with that mystery into which we can only dimly glance, they often do not profess belief in him. Blinded by "religion," we crucify these people and so they are able to gain the special place in the constellation of heaven for which they were handpicked.

I guess the marvellous thing about it all is that, incapable of "religious" feelings, they will be completely surprised at the heavenly feast that awaits them. The most beautiful part of my life as a priest has been the opportunity my travels and assignments have given me to meet so many of these favored sons of a God who is full of surprises and who does not intend to be frustrated by those religious people who have as their profession "following his will." These "radicals" will experience salvation in an act of completely unanticipated ravishment that will usher them into the presence of the Living God. They are the Simone Weils of this world and they take heaven by storm and yet completely, as they will judge it, by accident.

Cheddi Jagan was born on March 22, 1918, at Port Mourant, a sugar plantation in the eastern Berbice section of Guyana. An early addiction to study brought him eventually to Howard University, in Washington, where he spent the years 1936–1938. He supported himself by taking jobs as a tailor and night elevator operator. He completed his studies at Northwestern University, in Evanston, near Chicago, graduating from its Dental School in 1942. During the time spent there, he met the one great romance of his life, Janet Rosenburg, a student nurse, who was a busy activist in leftwing causes. In the mysterious way in which lovers become united in mind and body, Janet became Cheddi and Cheddi became Janet and their individual fervent desires to work for social justice became one single driving force, which has motivated their lives ever since. Theirs is a great love story and a study in singleminded dedication to the ordinary person. In his book *The Middle Passage,* the great Trinidadian writer V. S. Naipaul describes a visit he made to Janet's office when she was Minister of Labor, Health, and Housing, in Cheddi's government:

> The side door of [her] office opened, and Cheddi Jagan himself came in. He was wearing a suit and carried a briefcase. He had just come in to say that he

The Decline of a Marxist

was off to the bank to sign the agreement for the loan to buy over the Georgetown Electric Company. It was an oddly domestic scene and I felt an intruder.

Janet Jagan lost her American citizenship for participating in Guyanese politics. Isn't it ironic and evidence of a topsy-turvy world that an American who has dedicated her life to the social betterment of a Third World nation should be deprived of her citizenship, while American businessmen who spend their lives raping the poor in economically underveloped nations are honored at the White House?

Those who point to Salvador Allende as the first self-proclaimed Marxist to come to power by the ballot box have overlooked the fact that Cheddi Jagan did so in the 1953 Guyana elections based on universal suffrage, in a sweeping victory with eighteen of the twenty-four seats in the Guyanese Lower House of Assembly. Along with six other members of his People's Progressive Party who helped form the Executive, Jagan promptly initiated legislation for the secularization of the schools, the strengthening of sugar-worker unions, and more direct taxation. The British Government, aghast at the prospect of a government dominated by a self-proclaimed Marxist, quickly put aside its pretence of approval of democracy and sought an excuse to destroy this democratically elected government. It found its excuse in Jagan's espousal of the secularization of the schools. With great self-righteousness, the Constitution was suspended "to prevent Communist subversion of the Government." PPP leaders (including Jagan) were detained and political meetings were banned. The hypocritical and dictatorial nature of the act was highlighted by the fact that the Colonial Office itself had previously recommended, not long before, that the schools be secularized.

The arbitrary suspension of the Constitution of a legitimately elected government on the grounds of saving democracy was perhaps not the most severe blow that Jagan suffered during this time. After all, Jagan knew that Britain's days as a colonial power in Guyana were numbered and, in jail or outside of jail, he alone commanded the allegiance of the vast majority of the Guyanese people. His greatest political setback and personal tragedy came, not from the British Government, but from his trusted aide, long-time friend, and deputy of the party, Forbes Burnham. Burnham left the PPP on the grounds that Jagan was a Marxist. Considering the fact that Forbes Burnham himself espoused Marxism, this reason for his departure evidently masked his intent to challenge Jagan for power. Ingratiating himself with Britain and aided by CIA activity in the unions, Burnham was asked by Britain to form a government after the December 1964 elections, in which the voting had gone along racial lines, the blacks voting for Burnham and the Indians voting for Jagan. The previous nonracial alliance had been shattered by Burnham's departure from the Party. Burnham had deserted ideology, made a quick grab for power and succeeded.

How hurt must have been his friend of many years when Burnham, in a speech in New Amsterdam, referred to Janet Jagan as, "that little lady from Chicago, an alien to our shores." The shared sacrifices, intimacies, study, friendship in London, where Burnham and Jagan had spent so much time preparing for their entry into Guyanese politics, had been dissolved in the acidity of a deteriorating comradeship.

No one was more outraged by Burnham's "treachery" than Edith, a long-time friend, supporter, and hostess for both Burnham and Jagan during their London days. Edith is a Communist. She was, when I was her friend, a Stalinist, a devoted and dedicated advocate of the policies of Moscow. With great vigor and yet, showing deep-

The Decline of a Marxist

seated signs of disappointment, she defended the Russian right to enter Czechoslovakia and the obviously unjust removal of Mr. Dubcek as he had scarcely begun a period of hopeful springs in his beloved nation.

Edith's influence, together with that of Janet Jagan, helped shape Cheddi Jagan's Marxism into the rigid form which was to bring about his eventual demise as an effective West Indian leader. But that rigidity was to come later. In many all-night sessions at Edith's modest London flat, Jagan stressed nonalignment, a policy later suspect at the State Department when Jagan attempted to develop his government policies in the face of furious onslaughts by nervous American and British governments. Burnham shared their company, their modest means, and the make-shift beds in the tiny living room. But Cheddi's idealism was seen by Burnham as a serious obstacle to holding power in a world dominated by British and American might. Cheddi's honesty could not be believed by cynical civil servants in the upper echelons of the Colonial Office and the State Department. Burnham decided to play the game. His Marxism became a slippery form of socialism. His earlier abhorrence of the politics of domination became a fascination of how it could serve his own ends. He set aside his earlier naiveté, shared with Jagan, that a program designed to bring his nation out of its historical dependency on foreign capital would meet with approval from men of good will in the developed world. Jagan continued to believe that the world would listen to an honest man with an honest program to help underdeveloped peoples attain dignity. Burnham knew that, in fact, this was exactly the kind of person that had to be eradicated. Burnham had discovered the secret of political success and he was to triumph over his mentor.

Edith arrived at Vivian's while I was still watching the Wimbledon matches. Her husband, Freddy, a black

Guyanese, was with her. We would all drive out to Heathrow airport that evening to greet Cheddi, who was scheduled to arrive at about 7 P.M. on a flight from Moscow. Edith was all agitation. Cheddi had always been, for her, the greatest leader in the Third World. His departure from power at the hands of foreign agents and the "usurpation" of power by Forbes Burnham, a "traitor," a man who had "sold out" the Guyanese revolution to satisfy his own personal ambitions, was more than she could handle. Edith, a very talented lady, had lost many an opportunity to make a good living because of her openly proclaimed Marxism and her open approval of Soviet policy decisions. Moscow was still, to her, the Mother of Communism. It never occurred to her that her influence on Cheddi's thinking may have had more to do with his losing power than even the cleverness of Forbes Burnham.

She was not a believer in flexibility, even though she managed to be quite flexible where Soviet policy would flip-flop on any given subject. She lived poorly and supported her husband, a quiet, untalented man whom I am sure she loved dearly, but probably married to show her solidarity with the Guyana of Cheddi Jagan. She was rather heavily in debt, but tried to survive from the income of her tiny off-set printing press. She would no sooner get an order than a rival would tip off the customer that Edith was a "dirty Communist," and a phone call would notify her that the order was being cancelled. I had spent a few afternoons in her shop helping out, and it was obvious that, more and more, the only customers she could hold on to were small radical groups that wanted a two- or three-page pamphlet printed. And, of course, they wanted reduced rates from a comrade. It was pitiful, but she was as holy as Saint Francis in her dedication. I, for one, would not hesitate to pray to her when she dies.

The Decline of a Marxist 109

Edith ran out to the lawn to find me, gave me a big kiss, and turned off my TV set with "the hell with that garbage." I had to read the match result in the newspapers that evening.

There was great excitement in the Cuppage home that afternoon as the dining room and living room were prepared to receive the distinguished guest. We made plans to pick up Mr. Jagan at the airport. A wealthy West Indian barrister, a close personal friend and supporter of Cheddi Jagan, provided the use of his Rolls Royce for Cheddi's visit. At Heathrow airport we noted the inevitable presence of C.I.D. people, keeping tabs on Cheddi's movements in Britain and on those who would be visiting with him. The intelligence information gathered by the British C.I.D. is shared with their counterparts in friendly countries. Upon my return to Grenada a few weeks later, I was informed by a member of the Grenada C.I.D. who was sympathetic with the local Black Power opposition movement that details of my meeting with Jagan had been received from London by Grenada security police. Included in that report was information on a visit I had also made to the Cuban Embassy during the same week. This did not bother me since I was under constant surveillance in Grenada by the Gairy government (Gairy was deposed in March of 1979 by Maurice Bishop, former Black Power leader and, more recently, leader of the opposition), and was often harrassed there by the police.

Jagan's plane from Moscow was right on time, and we all headed straight for the Cuppage residence. Cheddi was immaculately dressed, as always, and looking as fresh as if he were starting out to his Georgetown office at nine in the morning. I was struck by Jagan's handsome and kindly face. He is five feet seven inches tall, with brown eyes and greying hair and, in spite of his handsome looks and elegant dress, one is immediately at ease in his presence. His eyes betray his constant search for dialogue. He speaks English in flowing and elegant phrases and has a great command of his subject matter, whether it is economics, religion, or cultural identity. Jagan would be completely at ease in the most sophisticated upper-class salons in London, Paris, or New York. But he remains, always, a man of the people and can suddenly switch from complicated economic theory to a discussion of mundane farming methods. Naipaul quotes Jagan as he has a discussion with a farmer of Port Mourant:

> You work hard at your land, you been keeping your wife and five children now and you don't see why the Government or anybody else should come and tell you what to do or where to tie your young cow. Good. We know you work hard. But tell me . . . Who rice land your cows does mash down? And where you does pump your water out? In the next man land, not so? So, what about him.

For sheer delight no dinner has ever matched dinner with Cheddi Jagan. He smiled constantly; he explained with great patience and with the art of an excellent teacher some of the more complicated interactions of international power and intrigue. The amazing thing about Jagan is that he knew exactly how to stay in power; he knew exactly what to say, who to talk to, what concessions to make, what pretence with which he should associate himself. He would have, if he had tried even a little bit, outmaneuvered and out-classed Forbes Burnham. Knowing full well the consequences, he chose not to take this path. I am not sure he was right, as idealistic as it sounds. Humanly speaking, at least, it would appear that had he

The Decline of a Marxist 111

been able to give more years at the helm of state, Guyana would have been all the richer for it. But maybe not. Burnham's traditional approach to politics does not seem to have done badly for his nation and we do not have the data that would be necessary to compare what is with what might have been if Jagan had played the game and remained in power. Of course, nothing is ever quite that simple. Jagan's Communist orthodoxy was bound to be a stumbling block to him sooner or later. Perhaps it might have led to an abandonment of the development of local culture and tradition, something which had to precede a concentration on economic affairs.

Given his sensitivity, intelligence, and understanding of the economic and cultural forces shaping the new Carribbean, his stubborn allegiance to Moscow is inexplicable. I think there were times when he saw Guyana as politically unique as a South American nation, since the composition of its population is, culturally, West Indian. He was aware that his nation was not "South American," but he was not sufficiently aware that the destiny of Guyana was intimately entwined with the islands of the Caribbean. It was this misjudgment, perhaps, that led him into thinking that, on its own, it could become Marxist and be absorbed in some way by Moscow. Guyana is a low coastal plain lying between the mouths of the Orinoco and the Amazon and is geographically distinct from the West Indian islands, but culturally and politically tied to them. Forbes Burnham understood this and used this connection to make himself "one of them." Jagan became more and more an outsider. Those in power in Moscow appreciated his fidelity but became increasingly aware that it was Forbes Burnham with whom they must deal. Moscow will always value Jagan as a true son of the Bolshevik Revolution, but they are understanding of the fact that this is a political liability in the West Indies, where the new generation of politicians has no more taste for neocolonialism than it had for colonialism.

As the dinner and conversation moved along, Cheddi turned his attention to the Black Power movement in the Caribbean. He knew that in these young people were the Caribbean leaders of the late 70's and early 80's. Black Power, in the context of the West Indies, is a determination to end the history of white domination. The destruction of the African way of life, black language and culture was so devastating and so complete that blacks in the West Indies denied that their roots were in Africa and thus lived in a cultural no-man's-land. But a new generation came along in the fifties and sixties and began to seek a way to move out from under the yoke of cultural, economic, political, and religious domination. Cheddi expressed the opinion, fully shared by myself, that these Black Power leaders would bring about a completely new political climate in the Caribbean. Its Socialist orientation is inevitable. He asked me if I could give him a list of names and relative positions of influence of various Black Power leaders in Saint Lucia, Barbados, Saint Vincent, Grenada, Trinidad, and Tabago. He intended to fly directly to Barbados from London, on an island-hopping visit to meet with as many Black Power leaders as he could in the hope of forming some sort of loose political alliance that would result in a common vision for the West Indies of the 1980's.

There was no doubt in his mind that he would eventually return as Prime Minister, believing as he did that Forbes Burnham would eventually out-do himself and be seen for the opportunist that he was. I did not share this view since I believed that Burnham more truly reflected where West Indians were, politically, at that moment in time, but I let that pass without comment. He went to great pains to explain that his opposition People's Progressive Party and his contacts with Socialists around the world could play a significant role in assisting the evolution of people who were destined for leadership. I felt uneasy about giving him names, but I did settle for giving him the names of a few people in Barbados whom he could contact and suggested that if his visits were successful and if they saw a value in expanding their contacts with him, then he could take it from there. I did warn him, however, that his open avowal of the Moscow brand of socialism placed him in a very weak position vis-à-vis the Black Power leadership, which was committed to the evolution of a local brand of socialism. He was difficult to dissuade and the attitudes and style he reflected made it easier for me to understand why he had become an honorable has-been in Caribbean politics. He was out of touch with reality and seemed unable to change an attitude and rhetoric that were no longer viable in the Caribbean. Forbes Burnham, on the other hand, understood the situation. However, this did not lessen my respect for Cheddi, and I wished this good man a pleasant trip to the islands.

True to the stubbornness that accompanies rigid adherence to ideology, it later came back to me that Cheddi did not call on those whose names I had given him and that his stay in Barbados convinced the local Black Power leadership that he was not a man with whom one could deal. He readily listened to a few young people who spoke the same ideological language as himself and was blind to the fact that, although he had come to Barbados specifically to meet some of the young people in the movement, these people he spent time with did not relate to it. Many of the Black Power leaders lived on the edge of incarceration all the time, and Cheddi showed a surprising lack of self-control in his talks and speeches, often publicly stating views transmitted to him privately. It was clear that he was not making any serious attempt to understand the local situations.

He repeated this error a few months later in the heat of the Grenada general election campaign when Unison Whitman, the editor of *Jewel,* the movement's newspaper, was challenging Prime Minister Gairy's wife in her home district. I received a letter from Jagan asking me to try to arrange for him to give two talks in Grenada on dates which happened to fall in the final week of the election campaign. I replied that his appearance to give a political talk during the final days of the campaign would give the impression that Unison (and by extension the movement) was being backed by Communists. Since, in fact, the movement wanted no such support, I advised him not to come because his visit would cause a lot of damage. We could reschedule him to speak at rallies at another time. To my great surprise, Jagan contacted a disaffected member of the movement privately and arranged to fly to Grenada in the final days of the campaign. I had previously discussed Jagan's requested visit with Maurice Bishop, then head of the Black Power movement and now Prime Minister of Grenada. Maurice was furious. All of us were stunned, and it was a clear signal to the leaders of the movement throughout the Eastern Caribbean that their suspicions of the motives of outside forces were well-founded. It was evident that Jagan wanted to use the local movement for his personal or Communist ends rather than in the service of the local people. From that moment on there was no possibility that his friendship or advice would ever again be of any consequence. As it turned out, the then Prime Minister, Eric Gairy, forbade him to disembark in Grenada when the plane arrived. Thus the entire episode was a personal disaster for him, and caused whatever credibility he had up to that time to evaporate. It all seemed so sad and stupid.

Jagan is, temperamentally, one of the old-time Marxists. Their days are coming to a close in Europe, in Asia, and even in Eastern Europe. Jagan is a beautiful man, a great personality, but he became the symbol of the decline of a particular form of the Marxist.

10
May Marx Rest in Peace

The scene at Highgate Cemetery on the outskirts of London was depressing. Eleven shivering people stood around an inexpensive casket on a damp, cold morning in March 1883. Only one of the deceased's children bothered to come to the funeral and of the eleven present, six were poor German emigrés. Karl Marx was about to be lowered into the cold ground and although he was one of the most controversial figures in Europe, his burial was almost completely ignored by the public. He had lived in London for thirty-three years but was almost unknown to Britains. The only mention of his death that appeared in the English press was a brief death notice penned, not by a local correspondent, but by the Paris correspondent of the *Times*. The deceased's major work, *Das Kapital,* had not as yet been published in English.

Like Christ, Marx lived in poverty and died in poverty, and again, like his Savior, it did not occur to anyone that Marx was to be the inspiration for a world-wide movement which was to radically change the way people thought and the way people lived. The Jewish historian, Josephus, wrote of Jesus that if his movement had any value it would grow and if it did not then it would die. An observer of the crucifixion, however, was more positive in his assessment: "Surely this was the Son of God." At Highgate Cemetery that cold March morning Friedrich Engels, Marx's friend and patron eulogized: "On March 14, at a quarter to three in the afternoon, the greatest living thinker ceased to think." Then Engels goes on to observe: "His name will endure through the ages and so will his work." Given the circumstances of his death, however, Engels' optimistic words appeared to be a bit of whistling in the dark. Nor was he given much of a chance by those prophets of later years. As recently as twenty years ago, Bishop Fulton Sheen said that in fifty years' time our children will ask, "What was communism?"

The good bishop assumed that communism could not and would not survive. In a sense, his prediction may, we pray, prove to be correct in reference to communism as a repressive dictatorship, but insofar as his prediction relates to communism as socialization, he is already proven wrong. Communism as socialization is the historical imperative predicted and yearned for in the Old as well as the New Covenants. It is only when this simple fact is understood that Marx will be seen in proper perspective by the Christian world. Marx had rediscovered the meaning of the Hebrew covenant with Yahweh. As Engels observed in the eulogy: "Just as Darwin discovered the law of the development of organic nature, so Marx discovered the law of the development of human history." Engels cried out with emotion as he stared at the casket lying on the frozen ground: "And so it happend that he was the most hated and calumniated man of his time." The similarity with Christ is again striking. St. Mark records the crucifixion scene: "And he was reckoned among the wicked."

The circumstances of Marx's death, the anonymity of it, the total and complete lack of public (even private) interest in it can help the reader to understand the real Karl Marx. The current portrait of him as the wild and ferocious leader of an active revolutionary party is refuted both by the thirty quiet years in a London ghetto and the unspectacular circumstances of his death. His revolutionary battles were fought for the most part from behind his desk, where he expended his life's energy studying and writing about the laws of human nature and the marketplace. What kind of man Marx might have been if in fact he had become involved in an actual revolutionary situation we can only speculate. But based on his super sensitivity to the alienations and sufferings of the common person to whom he dedicated his entire life, my own guess is that he would have been unable to stomach any form of violence. He died as he lived, with two particular charisms, his unusual brilliance of mind (perhaps the most brilliant in history) and his prophetic anger. "What the bourgeoisie, therefore, produces, above all, is its own gravediggers. Its fall and the victory of the proletariat are equally inevitable." His outrage stemmed from his keen insights into the oppression of the workingpeople.

It was in the England of Queen Victoria that Marx witnessed the ravages that industrialization can bring on society. Marx had perceived what he described as an inevitable progression from the alienation of an individual worker in industrial society, to the alienation of a class, the proletariat, and then, by way of the class struggle, to the inevitable revolution that would one day liberate all people from the suffering and alienation that had disfigured humanity.

Given Marx's prophetic role and his profound compassion for human sufferings, surely it could not be out of piety that people condemn and ridicule this giant of a man; it can only be the insecurity they experience at the prospect of the social changes implied in the truth he so eloquently expressed. The racism, exploitation, and sexual depravities so characteristic of the Western social classes and racial groups most bitterly opposed to the teachings of Karl Marx explode the myth that he is opposed on religious grounds. In fact, if Marx had been corrupt he would have been co-opted by them long ago. The hypocrisy of affluent and vested interests assuming a posture of righteousness when the name of Marx is mentioned is so massive and prevalent as to escape the notice of those who have grown up believing in, and praising as ideal, the exploitative society. Persecution based on self-righteous hypocrisy and ignorance is as much a part of religious teaching today as it was in the time of Joan of Arc. The difference is that such ignorance and hypocrisy has far less social effect in a more enlightened society that continues to move toward openness and honesty. The death knell for this kind of hypocrisy will be sounded when the institutional Church finally becomes conscious of the leading role it has played in buttressing the evil forces let loose in the capitalist society.

The real Karl Marx bore no resemblance to the fire-breathing atheist. He was very much the Victorian gentleman in his life-style and habits, excepting of course the Victorian narrowness of mind. From his habit of enjoying the excellent Bordeaux that he received from his friend, Engels, to the embossed stationery he often purchased for his wife, Marx was a poor English gentleman. One can hardly detect a home atmosphere of militant atheism, as his daughter Tussy writes to her sister Laura: "I am writing to you on Christmas Eve. I remember times when you and Jenny dressed dolls for me and times when there were Christmas trees."

His speculation on the stock market, his fondness for the fairy tales of Snow White and Noisy Goblin, his Sunday afternoon picnics with his children on Hampstead Heath, his playing the horse in horseback-riding games with Laura and Tussy, his gusty renditions of German patriotic songs portray the real Karl Marx. He was a family man, a gentle man who was inspired by God to denounce in a prophetic manner the obscenities, evils, and inconsistencies of runaway capitalism.

Tussy, of whom Marx said, "Jenny is most like me, but Tussy is me" did not hesitate to use the name of God as she rewrote Britain's national anthem on the occasion of the Fenian Insurrection in Ireland, in 1867:

> God save our flag of green
> Soon may it bright be seen
> God save the green
> Send it victorious
> Peaceful and glorious
> God save our flag of green
> God save the green.

The Victorian upbringing of Marx's children is further attested to by the fact that they did everything they could to hide the fact that a bastard son of Marx had surfaced. They feared the tainting of his reputation for intellectual honesty and personal integrity. Tussy, especially, was obsessed with this fear.

Marx was a theorist, a theorist with a difference. He differed from many another theorist precisely in the passion of his prophetic utterances and the incisive quality of his analyses. He inspired others to stop philosophizing about the world and get about the business of changing it. Surely no one before or since Jesus has had such a great impact on both the intellect and the emotions of human beings. That this great prophet was to be interpreted in many and various ways by those who claimed to be his true disciples was to become clear not too long after his death.

May Marx Rest in Peace

Rosa Luxemburg stood at the crossroads of three principal interpretations that tore the early Marxist movement apart. Luxemburg, who was born in Poland in 1870, twelve years before the death of Karl Marx, and who dedicated her entire adult life to moving Marx's dream one step closer to reality, strongly affirmed what is perhaps the most appealing concept of Marxism, that the revolutionary consciousness of the common person develops of its own accord from the inexorable forces of history. No leaders, no generals are needed to form the revolutionary consciousness. Their only function could be that of an enlightened directing of the powerful energies spawned by the inevitable revolutionary consciousness. Ideologically opposed to her were two intellectual giants in their own right. Eduard Bernstein, close friend and confidant of Marx's children, and Vladimir Ilyich Ulyanov (Lenin). Bernstein, observing that the prediction of Marx that the peasants in Europe would decrease in number and that the middle class would disappear was being contradicted by events in Europe, re-interpreted Marx's doctrine to be one of gradual reform and change.

Rosa Luxemburg attacked this "revisionism" with an audacity and clarity that startled the members of the German Social Democratic Party, the only well-disciplined and organized organization that European Socialists could look to for guidance. She declared that only a genuine revolution of the workers was radical enough to destroy the evils of the capitalist economic structure. Capitalism, she said, would not, could not, because of its inherent contradictions, reform itself. After effectively disposing of Bernstein, she threw down the gauntlet to Lenin himself. In this struggle, she came out second best and Lenin went on to be the man who was the first to apply the Marxian doctrine to the governing of a nation.

Luxemburg had faith that in time the proletariat would overthrow the system of capitalism in a massive insurrection. Lenin disagreed. He believed that only a proletariat led and directed by a specially-trained and elite vanguard, the Communist Party, would have the cohesion, the knowledge, and the tenacity to bring about a Socialist state.

Luxemburg, like Marx, was prepared to wait. The recent revival of Rosa Luxemburg's approach, especially among West European Marxists, may signal an approaching era in which an evolutionary approach to revolutionary consciousness may become popular. Once again the comparison between Marx and Jesus is inevitable. The gospel message has had a good deal of differing interpretation by sincere and dedicated people. The vision and gentleness of a Pope John XXIII has always been "balanced" by the harshness and narrowness of an Archbishop Lefebvre. And of course many crimes and atrocities have been committed in the name of both Marx and Jesus. Once a movement has been launched, there is no telling what kind of zealots will become attached to it and will attempt to use it as a vehicle for the expression of their own neuroses and lust for power. Lenin foresaw the use that Stalin would make of the Marxist movement and unsuccessfully tried to prevent his accession to power.

The persecution of Karl Marx is marked by about the same amount of insanity as characterized the defaming of Martin Luther King by the F.B.I. Anyone listening to the Congressional Subcommittee hearings on the role of the F.B.I. in the investigation of Martin Luther King would be alternately appalled and amazed at the answers given to committee investigators by F.B.I. officials. The man who was in charge of the Martin Luther King "operation" was asked why Mr. King's case was put under the heading of subversive activities. Did the F.B.I. have any evidence whatsoever to link Mr. King with any kind of subversive activity? The answer, amazingly, was no. Naturally the questioner then went on to ask why then Mr. King was investigated by this unit. The highly placed F.B.I. official answered that he had no idea and could give no reason why Mr. King was so characterized. He was then asked why it was that the F.B.I. had pictured Mr. King's movement as violent. After all, Mr. King was known all over the world for his advocacy of nonviolence. Once again the F.B.I. official said that he had no idea. Such an answer coming from the very man in charge of the operation was unbelievable. Finally, he was asked if it were not immoral for the F.B.I. to send Mr. King a tape on which they suggested to him that he kill himself. This F.B.I. official, who ranked third or fourth under Mr. Hoover himself, answered that he was not able to make a moral judgment on such a matter.

It is this same kind of irrational criticism and condemnation that has been heaped on Karl Marx, a man who stands head and shoulders above his detractors both morally and intellectually. What prompts this kind of insane behavior? Perhaps the clue lies in the answer the F.B.I. official gave when asked what Mr. Edgar Hoover thought of Martin Luther King. "He hated him," was the calm reply.

We Christians are guilty of gross character assassination. I don't know where we can make a start or how, but the more humane society, together with some effort to live up to the gospel message that we publicly adhere to, demands that we some day look at what Marx wrote and criticize it on the basis of logic, free from the debilitating effects of ancient prejudices and the lack of simple Christian charity.

11
Karl Marx and Religion

Despite everything, we can forgive Christianity much, for it has taught us to love children [Marx].

It is ironic that the tools of critical analysis and exegesis are diligently and artfully applied by theologians to the most obscure commentators of religious texts who touch only the lives of a tiny academic circle. At the same time they have largely avoided this kind of studied exegesis of context in the case of Karl Marx, a man who has had the most profound effect on the religious practice of humanity since Jesus Christ.

Marx was a religious man. It was in his blood. On both sides of his family he was a descendant of rabbis and rabbinical scholars going back to before the fifteenth century. The chief rabbi of Venice-Padua, in Italy, in the mid-1500s, Isaac Katzenellenbogen, was an ancestor of Marx. Virtually all the rabbis of Trier, where Karl Marx was born, were of his family. The interpretation of religion and religious values was part of his heritage and warmed his blood. Of course, one could hardly have expected Marx to have much respect for organized religion since his father, a lawyer, was forced to convert to Christianity. After the defeat of Napoleon at Waterloo, Trier became

Karl Marx and Religion 125

Prussian and the pious Protestant Prussian government passed a law barring non-Christians from practicing law. Marx himself, at the age of six, was forced to become a Christian by another decree that barred non-Christians from attending public schools. To further becloud his view of religion, the founder of the Church which operated the school the young Marx attended was Martin Luther. And it was on this very site that Luther preached the persecution and extermination of "this damned rejected race." It was here that Marx's own self-alienation began by his acceptance of the Jewish stereotype. He was to write later on:

> Money is the jealous god of Israel before whom no other god may exist. Money degrades all the gods of mankind — and converts them into commodities.

Marx is often portrayed as devoid of emotional feeling for Christianity. The opposite was true. His interest in things religious and his own religious values are revealed early in a paper prepared for the finals of the Gymnasium in Trier. The paper was entitled, "The Union of Believers with Christ, According to St. John's Gospel 15:1–14." In it he writes:

> Thus the union of Christ imparts a joyousness which the Epicurean in his frivolous philosophy and the deep thinker in his most arcane science have vainly tried to snatch at.

Some commentators say that Marx did not believe in what he was writing but wrote what he did to please his teachers. This could be so, I suppose, put I prefer to think that the intensity and idealism which all of his later writings were to reflect, together with his life-long habit of saying what he thought, makes this assertion very questionable. His entire life was living testimony to the fact that he saw the emptiness of material things and the vanity of the world, more than almost anyone who ever lived, perhaps more than anyone since Jesus. It is not surprising, therefore, that before he began to experience the very "human" way in which the institutional Church preached the gospel message, he had become fascinated by Christ and perceived correctly that union with Christ brought a fullness far transcending any earthly happiness or musings. I am sure he felt this way until the very end of his life, but to express himself in Christian terms would have been, for him, to succumb to and give further credence to the distortion and alienating tendencies of organized religion.

In his later writings his criticism of Christianity was always intimately connected with his criticism of the Prussian state. I doubt very much if Christianity would have come under fire except for the fact that the Prussian government defended its terrible abuse of civil rights and its incompetency by declaring that what it did, it did in the name of Christian civilization. Prussia claimed to be a Christian state and so an attack on Christianity was for the purpose of undermining the Prussian state. Marx put it this way: "For Germany, the criticism of religion is the premise of all criticism." Correctly understood, Marx was perfectly justified in his approach to the criticism of the government. That Marx believed, even for a moment, that the Prussian state reflected true Christian values is an idea that could not possibly be entertained.

Marx's ability to distinguish between religion and religious institutions is attested to by his passion for social, racial, and economic justice. In this he reflected the ancient Hebrew passion for peace and justice. It was in his bones and no amount of rejection of formalized religion ever, even for a moment, caused him to become in any sense of the word "worldly" or nonreligious. He lived and died a model of Judeo-Christian values. Of course, in the minds of many, one cannot be religious unless one belongs to an institution and unhesitatingly defends every aberration of religion and religious values in the name of loyalty. Marx admired the American situation:

> In the United States there exists neither a state religion nor a religion declared to be that of the majority. ... The state is foreign to all cults.

But Marx does go on to observe that

> [the United States is] pre-eminently a land of religiosity, where none believes that a man without religion can be an honest man.

His constant abstraction of religion from the way it is practiced is evidence enough that Marx had no objection to religion, but only to its use as a tool of domination, superstition, or exploitation. The fact that such negative attributes could be predicated of religious institutions kept him at arm's length from them for all of his adult life. But his impact on religious institutions has been tremendous. His writings have brought about the deepest soul-searching among people of every land about the content and value of the Christian faith. His observation that Luther shattered faith in authority because he restored the authority of faith is not the statement of a man ignorant of things religious. Marx's great theological contribution is that he has set the stage for the secular *oikoumene*.

The religious ecumenical movement of our time has concerned itself with the breaking down of artificially created borders among the Christian peoples. This was long overdue but contains little of theological substance.

It helps get the Christian house in order but it does not, of itself, move Christian institutions away from the dead center of their narcissistic preoccupation with personal salvation. But since it is not until the Christian house is in order that the Christian churches will generate the intellectual creativity needed for the next major advance in human development, the Christian ecumenical movement has been a necessary prerequisite. The Christian world is preparing itself for the coming of the secular *oikoumene*.

The secular *oikoumene* will have as its objective a reconciliation of Christian and atheist dogmatism. This is where the true theological center must be. Until it reaches this point, theology will continue to be the irrelevant discipline which it is today. Certainly, the Catholic hierarchy, to their credit, have for some years now emphasized the importance of the practical (pastoral) over the theoretical. The spectacle of theologians and liturgists preoccupied with innovative changes in liturgy, while the world is beset with many intractable economic and social problems, has brought about the current low esteem in which the theological disciplines are held. The modern theologian lives in a world of introspective discussions of married clergy, women priests, communion in the hand, communion under both species, etc., etc., etc. The sad state of theology has to do with the fact that, for all its academic brilliance, it now deals with a refinement and a re-refinement of the superfluous at that. When theologians become aware that the resolution of the Christian-atheist impasse now awaits their theological attention, then shall theology reinvigorate itself and the Christian world will continue its significant march through history.

At this juncture of history, the exciting thing that is happening is that Marxists and Christians are becoming aware that their philosophies are most certainly not antagonistic but necessary complements, desperately in need of merger. The insertion of Marx into theology and the insertion of Jesus into Marxism is both the challenge and the hope of the future. It is this for which the world groans in anticipation.

Marx's preoccupation with religion is a thread that weaves in and out of his works. He defends Epicurus against the charge of irreligion, finding in his doctrine of the eternity of atoms an affirmation of the immortality of the individual self-consciousness. In defending Epicurus he even quotes the seventeenth-century mystic Jakob Böhme for support: "Whoever conceives eternity as time and time as eternity is freed from all discord." His reflections, given in great detail, on the contrast and parallel between Platonism and Christianity is further evidence of the intense desire he had to probe the relationship between religion as God, as rite, as morality, and that complex pulsating consciousness which is human life.

That Marx was concerned not with the destruction of religion but with a historical analysis of how religion has become incarnate in society becomes clear in his criticism of Christianity. The pre-Christian era, he says, was characterized by the bondage of nature. Even the gods in their heaven were nothing more than glorified human beings with all the vices and imperfections of their human friends who lived below. The pre-Christian world longed for liberation from this bondage and looked in anticipation for the infusion of a spirit untrammeled and unsoiled into the body politic. This spirit would liberate, lighten, purify the world from its own uninspired flesh. It was, then, a great moment in human history when Christianity raised a dying humanity from the sepulcher and tore the chains off a spiritless nature in bondage. The opportunity for producing a harmonious duality between spirit and nature had arrived at the given historical moment of the birth of Jesus, the Christ. But the promise was to remain unfulfilled, the yearning frustrated. In time, the Christian spirit became frozen, rigid. In the unchanging Word of the canonized Bible, a congealed tradition became the new instrument of tyranny and suppression more dangerous than a lifeless nature in bondage, because it was more refined and more readily accepted and identified as spirit. The task of the modern world, for Marx, is to melt down the frozen spirit and release it once again in an opportunity to fulfill its original function.

Marx's criticism of the popular conception of God in no way proves that Marx did not believe in God, but rather that he did not believe in the God as described by the Christians of his time. Theirs was a petty god before whom one must tremble and for whom one must abandon all worldly concerns and an involvement with human destiny. This abandonment was called perfection. Self-alienation, therefore, becomes the *sine qua non* of perfection. He sets forth his criticism in the *Critique of Plutarch's Polemic against Epicurus's Theology*. The name of God always arouses in the people, he says, fears of all kinds and causes them to be constantly engaged in a moral introspection that attempts to discover if this act is good or bad, if it is deserving of heaven or hell. Guilt and remorse are the consequences of their belief. If our morality depends on the whims of such a capricious God, then we can never be confident that we are fulfilling our duty to God, to others, or to ourselves. We remain so preoccupied with securing our own salvation that we have neither the time nor the inclination for the building up of the world about us. This causes us to become dead to ourselves; we become self-alienated. We fear the divine forces over which we have no control, but which control our every act. There is plenty of room left in the soul of Marx for a belief in a God who is not a reflection of this popular image.

Marx then goes on to examine the ontological proof for the existence of God put forth by some scholastic philosophers and by Hegel himself. From the thought of God's existence, we can conclude that God does exist. Marx simply observes that if the ontological proof is valid, then we would have to conclude that Moloch, the Canaannite god, and Apollo, the Greek god, actually existed. Of course, if the god of a Germanic tribe were transported to the land of the Greeks or the land of the Canaannites, the Germans would have discovered the nonexistence of their gods because the Greeks and the Canaannites would consider the German gods as nonexistent. So, prescinding from an objective existence of God, Marx demonstrates the weakness of the ontological argument. Gods do exist for those in whose imagination they are real. For the rest they do not exist. The criticism of the popular concept of God, then, is not to be interpreted as "atheism," but rather as a methodology to which Marx is consistently faithful. He focuses on the relationship of religion to the world, humanity, and society. He leaves the study of religion as a psychological or mystical phenomenon to others, except in those areas in which he discovers fraud or misuse. But religion relates to the world because it receives its reality from the world.

Marx was not interested in opposing the tenets of Christianity with the tenets of atheism. He sees the propagation of atheism as a waste of time. The atheists use the negation of God as a basis for affirming the independent existence of humankind. This kind of atheism no longer has any meaning because it is not necessary to deny the existence of God to affirm, as socialism does, that positive human self-consciousness is the vehicle of human development. One does not have to start a war with God to establish this fact. Marx always believed that militant and propagandizing atheism was unnecessary at best and stupid at worst.

On more than one occasion, Marx attacked with particular zest those who attack Christianity. He published an article in the New York Communist newspaper *Der Volks-Tribun*, attacking the editor, Hermann Kriege. Kriege boasted that he was an atheist and, according to Marx, "tries to bring out various infamies of Christianity under the protective shield of communism." Marx was never superficial, and any unfair or ridiculous attack on Christians or Christianity was certain to be rebuffed by him in the strongest language.

The common understanding of Marx's attitude toward religion is, in fact, not Marx's at all but rather that of Marxist-Leninism as developed by the Soviet Communist Party. Following what he knew was the mind of Marx, Lenin declared freedom of conscience in the Soviet Constitution. But his later actions and his antireligious crusade in Russia recast the ideological function of the Party as envisioned by Marx and Engels. It was Stalin who carried Lenin's policy to its logical conclusion when he asserted on the one hand that the Soviet Constitution permitted all citizens to profess the religion of their choice and also safeguarded the right of every citizen to combat any and all religions. That this attitude was diametrically opposed to everything Marx and Engels believed was dramatically illustrated in Engels' sarcastic attack on Karl Dühring, a positivist philosopher who saw the principle of socialism to be anticlericalism:

> But it does not matter what we want. What matters is what Herr Dühring wants. . . . A socialization system rightly conceived, has therefore . . . to abolish all the paraphernalia of religious magic, and therewith all the essential elements of religious worship. . . . He out-Bismarcks Bismarck. He decrees . . . not only against Catholicism, but against all religion

whatsoever [*Marx and Engels on Religion* (New York: Schocken Books, 1974), pp. 147, 149].

Marx thought that religion was going to die anyway. We cannot (or rather, do not) agree with Karl Marx, but it could just be that religion as he knew it in his time is dying. Marx spells out his position on religion and the state very clearly in *On the Jewish Question*. He believed in the separation of Church and state. Marx speaks of the emancipation of the state from religion and is therefore sometimes interpreted as advocating the opposition of the state to religion. As we saw above, Marx consistently opposed any interference by the state in matters religious. For him, the emancipation of the state from religion occurs precisely at that point in time when the state ceases to recognize any religion as the religion of the state, perceiving itself only as state. Marx's position on Church-state relations is similar to that obtaining in the United States. He specifically states that even if the overwhelming majority of the citizens still feel obliged to fulfill their religious obligations after the Church-state separation is complete, they should be completely free to exercise this right. Religion is a private matter and not an object of control by the state. If Christians were as tolerant of Marx as he was of them, they would be much more Christlike.

12
Eurocommunism

The basis for Eurocommunism is the understanding among Western European Communists that the ideal state as envisioned by Marx has not become a reality in the hands of his disciples and admirers. There are a variety of reasons why it has not. I suppose one could start with the basic one, namely, that much is lost in the application of any theory to the real world of people and events. And also it is no secret that the Communist states, far from having the popular support that Marx said was the sign of legitimacy, have achieved power by the generous use of the bullet. History has given us ample proof that those who rule by force become, in the end, victims of their own isolation. The use of force is a political reality that produces social and ethnic unrealities. The decrees of the strong do not become anything at all if the content of those decrees violates basic instincts and ancient cultural patterns. The economic, social, and theological currents of centuries cannot be channelled and directed into a single flow in the twinkling of an eye. Communist leaders have sought unity but they have failed to bring it about. It is not communism as a political force that will bring about universal unity, not communism as we know it today. The Communist state is an external and temporary phenomenon; a reflection of the internal and permanent movement of socialization that motivates modern humankind.

Eurocommunism is the West European Communists' response to their awareness of the temporary nature of the present Communist state. Since France, Italy, Sweden, Spain, and Portugal are not Communist states, Communists from these nations are able to view the shortcomings of Eastern-bloc communism with an emotional detachment that the Soviets and others are incapable of having. Every establishment tends to perpetuate itself with false and self-serving statistics, reports, and evaluations. West European Communists, not having to defend the obvious deficiencies and even deformations of this temporary phase of communism, have learned what not to do if and when they come into power. To their credit, many of them have not allowed their attachment to Marxist principles to blind them to the defects of their ideological colleagues in the East. Eurocommunism is not a retreat from Marxism; it is a cautious retreat from the Communist state as it has developed.

The obscene excesses of Stalin and other Communist leaders quite naturally bring forth the questions: What went wrong? and, What lessons can we learn from all this? This task does have its difficulties and pitfalls, however. Any attempt to re-evaluate Marxist principles in the light of economic and social developments that have occurred since Marx and since Lenin brings the accusation of revisionism. Eurocommunists are having the same problem with outdated Eastern Communists as those who are making an honest attempt to carry out the directives of Vatican II are having with the followers of right-wing dissidents in the Church. But this is a problem they will have to live with. Lenin "proved" that Marx was out of date. Stalin "proved" that Lenin was dated. Khrushchev "proved" that Stalin was an animal, and the Soviet Government "proved" that Khrushchev was not a true Communist. And yet we go around with that silly fear of monolithic communism, as if it ever existed. A nice myth, that's all. And now, finally, the East European Communists are "proving" that the Eurocommunists are revisionists.

Eurocommunism wants to do precisely what needs to be done. It is determined, first of all (and this the West hesitates to believe), to defend and maintain the hard-won civil liberties and democratic institutions which are part of the historic achievment of humankind. To these they wish to add now the legacy of Karl Marx, a new economic and social dimension. They want to do this in such a way as to avoid the mistakes made in the East. For example, they see the possibility of a transition from capitalism to communism occurring without the period of the dictatorship of the proletariat. Of course, Allende tried this and failed. The rationale for the dictatorship of the proletariat was that those who have power will not relinquish it without a fierce struggle. So, the possibility of a counter-revolution must be avoided by crushing the unconverted. Euro-Communists believe that things have changed, that the benefits of Marxism can now be chosen without benefit of an elite vanguard, by an enlightened and educated populace. Perhaps, before long, their convictions will be put to the test. And how will they come to power? Through the ballot box. And how will they continue in power? Through periodic elections.

Is this, as the East European Communists allege, a dangerous revisionist approach to the acquisition of power? If it is, then East European Communists have been living a lie all these years when they asserted that the reason force was necessary in the acquisition of power was the ignorance and intractability of the capitalist class. The dictatorship of the proletariat was a necessary evil. The assumption has always been that if, therefore, the time should arrive when, because of the "good" example of the East European bloc, West Europeans and others freely chose to embrace socialism, the need for force and the rule by an elite vanguard would disappear. This was most certainly the position of Marx, who clearly stated that the sophistication of the populace in matters economic would lead to the dismantling of the state. The constant is that the dismantling of the capitalist socioeconomic structure can come about only through the direct accession of power. The variable is how power is to be attained. For Mao Zedong, power comes out of the barrel of a gun. It comes out of the barrel of a gun because it had to. It was the only way at his time, under those specific historical circumstances. The dictatorship of the proletariat, led by an elite corps, was a historical necessity. The overwhelming financial, police, and psychological power of the capitalist establishment made it inconceivable to Mao that there could ever be another way.

Fair enough. But if Marxists paid more attention to their own theory and had the same confidence that Marx had in the inevitability of socialism, many of the older Communist leaders would have understood that the socialization of humankind is a historical necessity that unfurls itself irrespective of either the brilliant leadership of the Communist superstars or the fierce opposition of the capitalist class. But, in the heat of battle, who has time for theoretical reflection? Of course, whether or not socialization has progressed to the point where power can be achieved by the education and persuasion of the majority is still an unknown. Allende thought the time had arrived. Perhaps it had, in Chile itself. I guess he did not add the CIA element into the formula for success.

Far from being revisionists, the Eurocommunists find plenty of justification for their stand in the writings of Marx and Engels:

> With the successful utilisation of universal suffrage . . . an entirely new method of proletarian struggle came into operation. . . . We can count even today on two and a quarter million votes. . . . To keep it intact until the decisive day, that is our main task [Marx/Engels, *Selected Works,* pp. 644 ff.].

The key phrase there is "until the decisive day." In the above context what could this mean except the day when they would win at the ballot box! Engels has rightly observed that universal suffrage had changed the picture. Prior to the winning of this important civil right, revolutions were merely the replacement of one small group in power by another small group in power. The average person had little or nothing to say and calmly acquiesced to the new rulers. Universal suffrage opens up the possibility that a revolution of economic or social habits can be accomplished with the approval and authority of the majority of the populace. Engels went so far as to say that the thinking of those who still favored engaging the military forces of the state in the streets was obsolete. I mention this not because he proved to be entirely correct (Castro, for example, reflected the majority wishes even though he used an elite vanguard to acquire power) but to show that the Eurocommunists have not departed from Marxist principles. They may, in fact, be striking much closer to its core meaning.

The proof of the validity of Marx's theory will not be demonstrated in the socio-political models of Eastern Europe, but in the success or lack of it of the new approach to power and socio-political activity now being planned by Marxists in Western Europe. Their criticism of their ideological colleagues in the East was a necessary first step in the construction of their own approach. Of course the fact of this criticism is something that, by itself, the Eastern Communists are furious about. It is unethical, they cry. It is hitting below the belt. It is giving comfort to the enemy. The Eurocommunists have broken the rules. They even state, to the dismay of the Soviets especially, that criticism will strengthen rather than weaken socialism, since if weaknesses are not openly discussed and analyzed they can lead to more general and debilitating problems. The old Communist leadership is having as much difficulty accepting this seemingly sensible position as are the conservatives in the Christian institutions in accepting a more humane Church legislation. Anyone familiar with both "institutions" would have no difficulty in believing that there is no difference in person-type between a bureaucratic Communist and an ultraconservative Catholic. They are interchangeable personality types. Apart from lip service, the average traditionalist Christian has no taste either for democracy or for the defense of human rights.

It rankles the East European leaders that West European Communists do not hesitate to say that the kind of socialism achieved thus far—which, by the way, they call "preliminary"—is not a shining example to be emulated. For the old-time Communists who struggled in what was a completely hostile capitalist world and who achieved a great victory in establishing a socialist state in the face of a powerful capitalist alliance, the Marxist dream has already arrived in and through their own personal struggle and triumph. They resent the new breed and accuse them of not appreciating what has been accomplished. It never occurs to them that they have been exaggerating what they have accomplished and have been equating their personal success with the triumph of Marxism. The Soviet Union is finding it impossible to get rid of its parent image and finds it completely unacceptable that other Communist states might not be completely dedicated to supporting and defending the parent-state of communism. The words of the leader of the Spanish Communist Party, Santiago Carrillo, are anathema to the Soviets:

> The role of the Communists in the West is not to strengthen the military bloc of the East; it is to carry out the political and social transformation in their own countries. . . . We want neither wars nor military defeats between the capitalist world and the socialist world [*Eurocommunism and the State*, p. 169].

13
The Economic Consequences of Marxist Ideology for the West

Mr. Codrington is (or at least he was, when I met him in London), the director of a very large diamond company having its principal investment in Sierra Leone, on the African continent. He was in an expansive mood. "It is principally a selling job or, as you Americans say, a snow job." Mr. Codrington was referring to the task he had set for himself during his upcoming trip to Africa. The next morning he was to leave London for Freetown, to have discussions with Dr. Siaka P. Stevens, President of Sierra Leone. It just happens that fifty-four percent of all exports from that African nation are diamonds. They are not only a girl's best friend in Sierra Leone; they are also its bread and butter. Mr. Codrington was, alternately, despairing and arrogant. He cursed the change in political climate that required as important a businessman as himself to "be summoned" by an African head of state to talk business. "Things are most certainly changing," he said, with an air of resignation. "But I might be able to talk him out of it." "Him" was President Stevens and what Mr. Codrington had to "talk him out of" was the President's insistence that there be much more local participation in the company's operations and ownership.

Sierra Leone became a British protectorate in 1896, and it was nigh impossible for a British businessman in 1971 to think of Sierra Leone as anything but a protectorate, even though the political situation had completely changed in 1967, when Sierra Leone became an independent nation. Adding to his wounded pride was the fact that Mr. Codrington did not consider himself to be just another businessman. "The Codrington family," he emphasized, "have always balanced their economic interests with support for established religion." And he was quite correct. In Bridgetown, Barbados, there is a lovely college called Codrington College. On its campus are trained the Anglican seminarians who are studying for the priesthood. Barbados is an Anglican stronghold and Codrington College an important and highly respected institution on the island. The family was not only a pillar of the Church there, but also of the society itself. It was important to Mr. Codrington to reflect the image of the good capitalist wherever he carried on his family enterprises. The following day he was to fly to Sierra Leone and be the tough but compassionate negotiator. I believe that he thought of himself as a kind of English Rockefeller.

Mr. Codrington had a plan. He would first insist, in his discussion with the President, that there be no changes at all made at the top levels of the company. He would warn President Stevens that if any changes were made, the company would face economic ruin and administrative chaos. He would hint that this in turn could result in his company's seeking another place to do its business. It was at this point, he believed, that the President would drop his insistence on local participation. And if his bluffing did not work, "What will you do then?" I asked. "I'll fight for every inch of ground and will retreat if necessary as far back as fifty percent local ownership." I then asked what would be his company's financial position if the President of Sierra Leone stood firm and won his battle for fifty percent local ownership. "We'd still make a lot of money," was Mr. Codrington's quick reply. In other words, if only half of the exploitation to which these companies were accustomed took place, there would still be a lot of money to be made.

This gives us some idea of the extent to which the African and other continents were raped of their natural resources. British diamond interests made countless millions of dollars mining in Sierra Leone, during the period of the British "Protectorate." While they filled the coffers of businessmen in Britain, the British administration did what was necessary to keep the nation at a survival level, but little or nothing more. One index of the quality of their "protection" is the statistic of the proportion of irrigated land area to total land area in Sierra Leone—0.011 percent. So long as there were enough natives to mine diamonds and bauxite (Sierra Leone is also one of seven nations that produce sixty-three percent of the world's bauxite), it mattered little to the British colonialists and Mr. Codrington's company whether or not the rest of the native population had even enough water to grow the crops on which their very physical existence depended. They just didn't give a damn. Sierra Leone was simply the place where English business mined diamonds and bauxite and the British "protectorate" was merely a police mechanism to see that it was done without interference.

I have not kept up with the fortunes of Mr. Codrington and his company, but it is likely that he is still doing well. He must be; I understand that he and his family are still very generously helping to produce Anglican clergy in Barbados. But his sons will not do as well, as more and more Third World nations become aware of the value of their natural resources and the absolute need that the developed world has for them.

An imperceptible but steady noose is being drawn around the economic neck of capitalist society and, barring a dramatic ideological shift to the left on the part of the West, this society is destined for economic strangulation. Perhaps "imperceptible" is not quite the right word, since one can hardly not notice the inflationary impact of the rise in OPEC oil prices. And yet, the rise in OPEC prices is not really quite germane to the destruction of the capitalist economies because these changes have been based on the shifting of political power, not on ideology.

The OPEC nations began their onslaught in the traditional capitalist manner, by creating a sellers' market out of a buyers' market. A buyers' market is one in which the sellers are disposed to accept a low price for their goods and services because of some external factor or factors beyond their control. In the case of the OPEC nations under colonialism, the external factor beyond their control was the political power of the colonial governments. They had no choice but to sell at the price determined by the "home" government. A sellers' market is one in which sellers are disposed to hold back their goods and services rather than sell them at a low price, and the buyers have a need for those goods and services in spite of the high prices. And so OPEC, now free of the colonial governments, can command high prices because, not only do they now control their own natural resources, but they have also come to an understanding of their value and the need that the West has of them. The buyers' market has now become a sellers' market. There has been no ideological shift, but simply a bit of education and a change in political power. The capitalist market conditions have remained.

The price structures of commodities such as oil had always been determined in London, Paris, or New York.

There was no "reason" why such price structures should have been created and manipulated in foreign capitals, but that's the way it was. There existed a kind of self-destructive innocence and naiveté in the underdeveloped world that arose, not so much from the military might of the West, as from the kind of trust and friendliness that is a natural characteristic of societies which have not as yet discovered the sins peculiar to a culture which is based on the economic imperatives of the profit-oriented society.

The Arabs, Africans, and Indians could have begun to put an end to the exploitation of their labor and their natural resources long before they actually did but (unbelievable as it may sound to cynical Westerners) it never occurred to them that the whites intended to exploit them, especially when they carried the cross. Exploitation was not really a significant part of their life-experience. Their sweet innocence would be defined by contemptuous Westerners as gullibility, but if gullibility is properly understood as a factor of exploitation then Westerners should feel shame rather than contempt. The con-artists from the West had actually convinced the Third World peoples that by exploiting their natural resources they (the con-artists) were helping them to become as advanced and as rich as themselves. They convinced the innocent native people that oil was not important; refineries were. Bananas were not important; banana flour was. Cocoa trees were not important; chocolates were. Too, they (the con-artists) took the oil and the cocoa and the bananas and the sugarcane, and sold it all back to the natives in little blue or white or brown boxes. This made everybody happy. The con-artists were happy because they were getting rich, and the natives were happy because they thought they were going to get rich. But even the smartest thieves make a mistake eventually.

The colonialists made their mistake when they decided to educate a few of the native elite. Their rationale was that by educating a few of them and setting them up as puppets in the government, they would minimize the possibility of future revolutions of liberation. The plan worked beautifully—for awhile. But gradually (to the dismay of the colonialists) the natives came to a realization that it was their natural resources, not the stuff in the blue, white, and brown boxes, that was valuable. The Africans came to realize that without cocoa and sugar, bauxite, gold, and diamonds, the West would be nearly broke. Once this realization sank in, the natives made plans to rid themselves of the con-artists from the "mother countries." It became obvious that these were "mother" countries who ate their young.

This almost universal awakening took place in Africa and Asia in the late fifties and early sixties. The outrage at having been lied to and cheated by "Christians" became such a torrent of protest that political power returned to the natives rather quickly. From that time on political power has gradually brought about more and more control of the economic power, true freedom.

The OPEC prices have been the most dramatic declaration of independence since the American revolution. It was a public declaration that the affluent capitalist societies have enjoyed their affluence not, as the conventional wisdom has had it, because of superior intelligence, but rather because they have been exploiting the natural resources of two-thirds of the world's population.

The well-trained elite, after attaining independence, put their newly acquired knowledge and financial expertise to use immediately. They had already learned that exploitation can extend far beyond the harem and the cow herd. Big bucks could be made from oil, sugarcane, bauxite, diamonds, and gold. The Arab sheiks began to exchange camels for Cadillacs and tents for Manhattan townhouses. In Arab, as well as other former colonies, the new elite had to put distance between themselves and the former colonial oppressors. They needed the right political weapon and they found it in Marxist propaganda.

Marx diagnosed, in boring but brilliant detail, the evils of the capitalist system, and the growing establishment of Marxist regimes in Asia and Africa gave promise that the egalitarian way of life could be achieved. And so, using the Marxist language of liberation, a tiny segment of the oppressed became the oppressors in their native lands. While maintaining and even increasing the level of oppression experienced under the colonialist administrations, the well-trained elite maximized the usefulness of Marxist propaganda and rhetoric. Echoes of the past, for Christian princes did the same thing in their day. They used the gospel according to Jesus to dominate, exploit, and abuse their subjects. Now it was the gospel according to Marx. Heavily cadillacked sheiks held news conferences condemning the oppressive economic policies of their former colonialist rulers and they assured their starving and naked populations that these foreign oppressors would never again be allowed to exploit them. Prudently, they refrained from saying that they themselves would now take care of that. Having learned the exploitative techniques of capitalist society and the rhetoric of the Marxist society, they have been enjoying the best of both worlds, and the adulation of a grateful populace which has canonized them for ridding the land of the hated capitalist oppressors. Take this statement of the former Shah of Iran, for example, issued in 1970. Marx could not have said it better:

> Developing countries producing raw materials are, as a rule, backward . . . and their economic growth is nil or a minus quantity.
>
> The reason for this is that the prices of the raw materials they export drop year by year at the whim of the consumer countries. . . . So, the backward or

developing countries grow steadily poorer while their populations increase in size, the prices of raw materials they export drop, and the prices at which they have to purchase their requirements rise. This state of affairs cannot continue [U.N. doc. St/ESA/27].

What the former Shah of Iran did not realize is that the people of Iran would agree with him. The Shah was one of the first big ones to fall; others will follow. All the Third World nations are becoming politically sophisticated and they observe what their politicians are doing with much greater awareness of the economic consequences of political acts. Thanks to Marxist terminology, they have been given a set of guidelines with which to measure their exploitation. No religious institution has done more for the people of the world than have the writings of Karl Marx. To him they owe their great awakening. And now that the peoples of the world are aware of the value of their natural resources, the real economic crunch on the West is about to begin.

The inflation now being experienced by the West as a result of the increase in OPEC prices will soon be eclipsed by inflation of enormous proportions. The reason is that, in spite of the change of economic and political masters, the changes in the producing (primary products) countries have been, up to now, mostly cosmetic. The ideological system of capitalism has survived, with new masters at the helm, and so long as the system hangs on there is no real threat to the economic survival of the West. But when the cosmetic changes in the Middle East, Africa, and Asia are replaced by real changes, we shall experience an inflation and a shortage of resources that will threaten the very fabric of Western society as we have known it.

At the moment, the Saudi sheik who becomes wealthy selling us oil keeps real estate brokers in Manhattan and

Beverly Hills affluent. The Saudi government official who places an order for 100 or 200 F-15s causes armament makers and their employees untold happiness. This was also true in Iran, but now the Shah is gone and the cosmetic changes which took place during the liberalization period of his regime are now being replaced by the real changes that affect our economy directly. The economic threat of ideological changes now becomes closer and very real. It has been getting tough in a market-place affected by the cosmetic changes of people whom we have kept in power. It will be chaotic and very damaging in a marketplace affected by ideology. The "Russians" are indeed coming, but they are coming in the form of Marxist-inspired revolutionaries and leaders. This is vitally important to understand, and to understand quickly.

Our State Department and our business community have been so accustomed to playing the same game with different players that it will be very difficult for them to understand that it is no longer just the players who are being changed, but the very rules of the game itself. The Iranians now refuse to buy our products, refuse to sell oil to Israel, and are prepared to bankroll the P.L.O. This will eventually mean disaffection among the Saudis, the North Yemenites, the Jordanians, and the Kuwaitis. The rate of attrition in our export markets will become so high that our very economic survival will be at stake. And it is right here that we might make our final and fatal mistake. We might decide (our Secretary of Energy and Secretary of Defense have already so threatened) to defend our economic interests by the use of force. Gunboat diplomacy may once again rear its ugly head. If it does, we are dead. It is unlikely that we will be wise enough to choose the only viable alternative — a re-evaluation of our posture vis-à-vis Marxist ideology. Evidence that we shall not be psychologically prepared to defend our interests rationally and adjust to the realities of a Marxist-oriented world abounds everywhere, even among the most sophisticated and talented of our people.

The present capitalist system concentrates control and power in a few metropolitan centers, leaving the rest of the world a vast hinterland with little or no capacity to plan its future. It is Karl Marx who has provided the world with an economic alternative based on reason, self-discipline, and justice. It is his disciples who now wage war against greed and injustice. Marx called for a system of independent socialist states in which information and technology flow freely between countries, but capital does not. Capitalism by its very nature can never allow this to happen, for it would mean self-destruction. The economists and leaders of the Third World have come to understand this and so no amount of rhetoric will ever again fool them. There was a time when it was considered an honor and an economic windfall of major significance to welcome investments by multinational corporations. This attitude is dead in many parts of the world and dying in the rest. In Yugoslavia, for example, joint ventures with foreigners cannot be concluded in banking, insurance, domestic transportation, commerce, communal or similar public services, or any social activity except scientific research. Foreign employees can repatriate only fifty percent of their earnings and the foreign enterprise must either reinvest twenty-five percent of its earnings or place that amount on deposit with a Yugoslav bank. The ability of multinational corporations to exploit the Third World decreases as the self-esteem of the Third World, enlightened by Marxist ideology, increases.

Surely, the capitalist world, in spite of itself, is undergoing structural transformation because of the necessity of dealing with Marxist praxis. While disclaiming its distaste for Marxism, the capitalist world is moving inexorably in its direction. It has become increasingly clear that social consciousness and the penetration of Marxist ideology are directly related. This, more than any other factor or theory, lends credence to Marxist analysis and adds a moral dimension to Marxist ideology that gives it the authority to challenge the social morality of the Christian West.

The Christian institutions have always condemned exploitation, but they have always, at the same time, made it a sin to attack the sources of exploitation. Completely misunderstanding the nature of capitalism, Christian leaders have vainly called for its spiritual transformation. They do not understand as yet that what is essentially evil cannot be transformed. The morality of the Christian institution has become so saturated with the philosophy of capitalism that it equates capitalism with Christian morality and culture. It has called what is sinful, right, and what is right, sinful. The institution has become an uncertain trumpet in the fight for economic justice. A major voice of justice in the world today is Marxist ideology. It is sad, but true. Readers of the *Wall Street Journal* would surely ascribe the following statement to Karl Marx or one of his disciples:

> The decadent international but individualistic capitalism in the hands of which we find ourselves after the war, is not a success. It is not intelligent, it is not beautiful, it is not just, it is not virtuous . . . and it does not deliver the goods. In short, we dislike it and we are beginning to despise it ["National Self-Sufficiency," an article by Maynard Keynes, 1933].

There is a new theory being spread about the academic, political, and economic establishments in America. It hopes to compensate for the new economic realities and save America's role as the world economic leader. The new thinking states that the way to avoid catastrophic dislocations in the American economy as a result of Third World economic aggressiveness is to help the Third World improve its economic condition. This aid, it is said, will help to diffuse potentially dangerous social transformations. "Social transformations" is a euphemism for Marxist ideology. The theory runs something like this. Science and technology are the critical components in any Third World effort to create self-sustaining growth.

That the United States government agrees with this statement is shown in the creation, by President Carter, of the Institute for Technological Cooperation. The *New York Times* reported: "Congress is now considering the proposal." The purpose of the Institute is to direct the United States Government's efforts to organize America's scientific and technological might in the fight against world-wide poverty, ignorance, and disease. The new theory is supposed to differ from the policies we have been following in that we had previously been simply transferring technology to the Third World. This took place with little or no consideration to training local people themselves to use the new technology imported into their lands. The new theory finally admits this. Cadres of foreign technicians used to accompany imported technology, at a very high cost to the host government. It is now envisioned that more and more local specialists will work with the foreign experts and that this will eventually lead to the capacity of an undeveloped nation to analyze its own structural problems and then apply their newly-acquired scientific and technological expertise to choose specific technologies best suited to the local situation. The creation of this institute is a response to the uneasiness among our top government officials and business executives about the rapidly changing geopolitical scene. No less a person than Father Theodore Hesburgh of Notre Dame, makes explicit their uneasiness:

Our future economic security and physical well-being will depend on the ability to increase international trade, maintain stability, avoid inflationary moves that grow out of scarcity of food and resources, and meet global environmental and population pressures.

Father Hesburgh headed the American delegation to the United Nations Conference on Science and Technology for Development held in Vienna in August 1979. Father Hesburgh is a fine American and an internationally-minded citizen. We can rejoice in the fact that he continues to command the respect and confidence of our national leadership. But that Father Hesburgh is on the right track is another question. The "new" theory being advanced by the Institute is really nothing more than the old theory; the same old face lies beneath a new mask. The theoretical assumption (easily accepted by theorists and academicians) that the scientific and technological community will agree to do more than transfer technology to the Third World is the fatal flaw in the new theory. This is an impossibility, since it would kill the very goose (capitalism) that lays the golden egg (maximization of profits). Well-intentioned people, like Father Hesburgh, who are asked to sit on such commissions, boards, etc. are really used as pawns in a propaganda exercise that has as its objective throwing a smoke screen over the real intentions of business and government—exploitation. The colonialist exploiters did the same thing when they carried priest, cross, candle, and Bible on every mission of destruction. What the members of the Institute for Technological Cooperation must realize is that their real task is to defend an economic system already discredited in most of the world. The brutal truth is that their task is, not to help the Third World, but rather to employ a more sophisticated plan for exploiting it.

Telling it as it really is in the capitalist jungle, is the Institute for Constructive Capitalism recently funded by such bed-fellows as Mobil, Shell Oil, and Tenneco. It has as its ultimate goal: "To construct a modern ethical and philosophical basis for capitalism." Disappointed with the attitudes discovered in the academic community, big capital is getting fed up. Former Treasury Secretary William Simon questions whether "the largest of the free enterprise system [should] continue to finance its own destruction." The major corporations agree with him and have already funded 30 different academic centers which must "teach our way or do without the money." With these attitudes, we in the West are rushing full-speed into economic dislocation.

We need not be Marxists or Marxist sympathizers to recognize the economic consequences of Marxist ideology today. We serve our own best interests by an intelligent national dialogue on how to deal with them.

OTHER ORBIS TITLES

ANDERSON, Gerald H.
ASIAN VOICES IN CHRISTIAN THEOLOGY

"Anderson's book is one of the best resource books on the market that deals with the contemporary status of the Christian church in Asia. After an excellent introduction, nine scholars, all well-known Christian leaders, present original papers assessing the theological situation in (and from the viewpoint of) their individual countries. After presenting a brief historical survey of the development of the Christian church in his country, each author discusses 'what is being done by the theologians there to articulate the Christian message in terms that are faithful to the biblical revelation, meaningful to their cultural traditions, and informed concerning the secular movements and ideologies.' An appendix (over 50 pages) includes confessions, creeds, constitutions of the churches in Asia. Acquaintance with these original documents is imperative for anyone interested in contemporary Asian Christian theology." *Choice*

ISBN 0-88344-017-2 *Cloth $15.00*
ISBN 0-88344-016-4 *Paper $7.95*

APPIAH-KUBI, Kofi & Sergio Torres
AFRICAN THEOLOGY EN ROUTE

Papers from the Pan-African Conference of Third World Theologians, Accra, Ghana.

"If you want to know what 17 Africans are thinking theologically today, here is the book to check." *Evangelical Missions Quarterly*

"Gives us a wonderful insight into the religious problems of Africa and therefore is well worth reading." *Best Sellers*

"This collection of presentations made at the 1977 Conference of Third World Theologians reveals not a finished product but, as the title suggests, a process. . . .On the whole, the book is well written and, where necessary, well translated. It adds to a growing literature on the subject and is recommended for libraries seriously concerned with theology in Africa." *Choice*

ISBN 0-88344-010-5 *184pp. Paper $7.95*

BALASURIYA, Tissa
THE EUCHARIST AND HUMAN LIBERATION

"Balasuriya investigates...the problem of why people who share the Eucharist also deprive the poor of food, capital, and employment....For inclusive collections." *Library Journal*

"I hope Christians—especially Western Christians—will read this book, despite its blind impatience with historical and ecclesial details and balance, because its central thesis is the gospel truth: eucharistic celebration, like the faith it expresses, has been so domesticated by feudalism, colonialism, capitalism, racism, sexism, that its symbolic action has to penetrate many layers of heavy camouflage before it is free, before it can be felt." *Robert W. Hovda, Editorial Director, The Liturgical Conference*

ISBN 0-88344-118-7   *184pp. Paper $6.95*

BURROWS, William R.
NEW MINISTRIES: THE GLOBAL CONTEXT

"This is an exciting, informed, thoughtful, and ground-breaking book on one of the most vital and threatening issues facing the contemporary church. Father Burrows seeks effectively to show that the older forms of church and clerical life, developed in the West, are both irrelevant and stultifying when transferred *in toto* to the Third World, and that as a consequence, new forms of church and clerical life, forms still within the Catholic heritage to which he belongs and which he affirms, must be developed if the church is long to survive in that new World. Burrows makes crystal clear the need for more open attitudes towards the forms of church and clergy if the newer churches are to become genuinely creative forces in the Third World rather than lingering embassies from the First World. I found the work exceedingly stimulating and the approach fresh and open." *Prof. Langdon Gilkey, University of Chicago Divinity School*

ISBN 0-88344-329-5   *192pp. Paper $7.95*

CABESTRERO, Teofilo
FAITH: CONVERSATIONS WITH CONTEMPORARY THEOLOGIANS

"This book shows what an informed and perceptive journalist can do to make theology understandable, inviting, and demanding. These records of taped interviews with fifteen European and Latin American theologians serve two major purposes: we are allowed to eavesdrop on well-known theologians in spontaneous theological conversation, and we are introduced to new and stimulating minds in the same way."*Prof. D. Campbell Wyckoff, Princeton Theological Seminary*

Conversations include Ladislaus Boros, Georges Casalis, Joseph (José) Comblin, Enrique Dussel, Segundo Galilea, Giulio Girardi, José María González Ruiz, Gustavo Gutiérrez, Hans Küng, Jürgen Moltmann, Karl Rahner, Joseph Ratzinger, Edward Schillebeeckx, Juan Luis Segundo, Jean-Marie Tillard.

ISBN 0-88344-126-8   *208pp. Paper $7.95*

CAMARA, Dom Helder
THE DESERT IS FERTILE

"Dom Helder Camara of Brazil, is a Roman Catholic archbishop whose sense of God's presence breathes through every page. But there is a difference. For Dom Helder has found God's presence in the lives of the poor, in the voices of the oppressed, and he communicates this sense of God's reality very powerfully. He takes us on a spiritual journey that can be utterly transforming if we will risk opening ourselves to him. He is no pessimist; in a world that seems devoid of God's presence, Dom Helder insists that *The Desert Is Fertile*. He does not minimize the 'desert' quality of modern existence: the increasing gap between rich and poor, the insanity of the arms race, and the 'marginalization' of human life, by which he means our tendency to treat the majority of the human family as nonpersons, those who are pushed over to the edges of life and ignored. 'The scandal of this century,' he writes, 'is marginalization.' He reminds us that if to have too little is a problem, so is having too much. 'Poverty makes people subhuman. Excess of wealth makes people inhuman.'" *Christianity and Crisis*

ISBN 0-88344-078-4 75pp. Cloth $3.95

CARDENAL, Ernesto
THE GOSPEL IN SOLENTINAME I

"Farmers and fishermen in a remote village in Nicaragua join their priest for dialogues on Bible verses. The dialoguers discover Jesus as the liberator come to deliver *them* from oppression, inequality, and injustice imposed by a rich, exploitive class: they identify Herod as dictator Somoza. Their vision of the Kingdom of God on earth impels them toward political revolution. This is 'Marxian Christianity' not as abstract theory but gropingly, movingly articulated by poor people. Highly recommended to confront the complacent with the stark realities of religious and political consciousness in the Third World." *Library Journal*

ISBN 0-88344-170-5 Paper $4.95

THE GOSPEL IN SOLENTINAME II

"Volume 2 follows the pattern of the first volume: villagers in Nicaragua join their priest, Ernesto, in interpreting New Testament verses. These volumes offer a profound challenge to the Christian conscience, and insight into the recent uprisings in Nicaragua. Highly recommended." *Library Journal*

ISBN 0-88344-167-5 Cloth $6.95

THE GOSPEL IN SOLENTINAME III

"A continuation of guided discussions on Gospel passages by the peasant folks in the Central American village of Solentiname. Has a most refreshing outlook." *The Priest*
Fortunately, the manuscripts for this and the fourth volume were safely in Orbis' hands before Somoza's soldiers destroyed Solentiname.

ISBN 0-88344-172-1 320pp. Cloth $7.95

CARRETTO, Carlo

LETTERS FROM THE DESERT

"Carretto, a very active layman in Catholic Action in Italy for twenty-five years, gave it up at the age of forty-four to become a Little Brother of Jesus. He heard the call to prayer and went into the desert. After a while he began to jot down things. The book was an instant success in Italy where, since its appearance in 1964 it has gone through twenty-four editions. It has been translated into Spanish, French, German, Portugese, Arabic, Japanese, Czech, and now, gracefully enough, into English. I hope it goes into twenty-four more editions. It breathes with life, with fresh insights, with wisdom, with love." *The Thomist*
ISBN 0-88344-280-9   146pp. Paper $4.95

LOVE IS FOR LIVING

"This book is truly excellent. Because we are all, indeed, poor, weak and empty, this series of meditations aims right at the human heart and beautifully articulates what goes on there. Some of the chapters are simply brilliant!" *The Cord*
"This book is meant for slow, prayerful pondering—a page or two at a time. It would probably be of help to persons searching for a deeper meaning in daily life, as well as those seeking a better knowledge of the Bible." *Religious Media Today*
ISBN 0-88344-291-4   158pp. Cloth $6.95
ISBN 0-88344-293-0   Paper $4.95

SUMMONED BY LOVE

"Those of you who treasure Carlo Carretto's books will be pleased by his latest, *Summoned by Love*. The book is a sustained meditation based on a prayer of Charles de Foucauld known as the *Prayer of Abandonment to God*." *Sign*
"Disarmingly simple and direct, Carretto's reflections testify to his familiarity with Scripture, the Church Fathers, and the down-to-earth realities of daily living. For one who is so 'traditional' in his spirituality, many of Carlo Carretto's ideas could be labeled 'liberal.' His writings indicate that he is in the mainstream of what is, and has been, truly vital in the Church universal. This valuable and timely book offers encouragement and challenge for all seeking to live within the changing Church and to find hope and love therein." *Catholic Library World*
ISBN 0-88344-470-4   143pp. Cloth $7.95
ISBN 0-88344-472-0   Paper $4.95

IN SEARCH OF THE BEYOND

"This little book will spur the reader to find his Beloved in solitary prayer. Creating a desert place for yourself means learning to be self-sufficient, to remain undisturbed with one's own thoughts and prayers. It means shutting oneself up in one's room, remaining alone in an empty church, or setting up an oratory for oneself in an attic in which to localize one's personal contact with God." *Western Michigan Catholic*
"'To lead others to contemplation is the heart of the apostolate,' according to Carretto. Here are excellent reflections on Scriptural themes, both old and new." *Spiritual Book News*
ISBN 0-88344-208-6   175pp. Cloth $5.95

CLAVER, Bishop Francisco F., S.J.
THE STONES WILL CRY OUT
Grassroots Pastorals

"Bishop Claver is the gadfly of the Philippine Catholic hierarchy who persistently buzzes in the ears of President Fernando Marcos and all his toadies. The bishop's book is a collection of fighting pastoral letters to his congregation after martial law closed the diocesan radio station and newspaper." *Occasional Bulletin*
"His gutsy strength has made him a prophet against the repressive regime. Some of his U.S. colleagues could learn from him." *National Catholic Reporter*
ISBN 0-88344-471-2   196pp. Paper $7.95

COMBLIN, José
THE CHURCH AND THE NATIONAL SECURITY STATE

"The value of this book is two-fold. It leads the readers to discover the testimony of those Latin American Christians who are striving to be faithful to the gospel in the midst of a most difficult situation characterized by the militarization of society, the consequent suppression of public freedom, and violation of basic human rights. It also invites the readers from other cultural and historical contexts to seek in their own situations the inspiration for a real theology of their own." *Theology Today*
ISBN 0-88344-082-2   256pp. Paper $8.95

JESUS OF NAZARETH
Meditations on His Humanity

"This book is not just another pious portrait of Christ. Its deeply religious insights relate the work of Jesus as modern scholarship understands it to the ills of our contemporary world." *Review of Books and Religion*

ISBN 0-88344-239-6   *Paper $4.95*

THE MEANING OF MISSION
Jesus, Christians and the Waytaring Church

"This is a thoughtful and thought-provoking book by a Belgian theologian and social critic, who has lived and taught in Latin America for 20 years. His rich background in evangelization, both in theory and in practice, is evident throughout his book." *Worldmission*
ISBN 0-88344-305-8   *Paper $4.95*

SENT FROM THE FATHER
Meditations on the Fourth Gospel

"In a disarmingly simple and straightforward way that mirrors the Fourth Gospel itself, Comblin leads the reader back to biblical basics and in doing so provides valuable insights for personal and community reflection on what it means to be a disciple of the Lord, to be 'sent' by him." *Sisters Today*
ISBN 0-88344-453-4   123pp. Paper $3.95

FABELLA, Virginia, M.M. & Sergio Torres
THE EMERGENT GOSPEL
Theology from the Underside of History

"*The Emergent Gospel,* I believe, is an expression of a powerful and barely noticed movement. It is the report of an ecumenical conference of 22 theologians from Africa, Asia and Latin America, along with one representative of black North America, who met in Dar es Salaam, Tanzania, in August 1976. Their objective was to chart a new course in theology, one that would reflect the view 'from the underside of history,' that is, from the perspective of the poor and marginalized peoples of the world. Precisely this massive shift in Christian consciousness is the key to the historical importance of the meeting. The majority of the essays were written by Africans, a smaller number by Asians and, surprisingly, only three by Latin Americans, who thus far have provided the leadership in theology from the developing world." *America*

ISBN 0-88344-112-8   *Cloth $12.95*

FENTON, Thomas P.
EDUCATION FOR JUSTICE: A RESOURCE MANUAL

"The completeness of the source material on the topic and the adaptability of the methodology—stressing experiential education—to groups at the high school, college, or adult levels make this manual a time and energy saving boon for most anyone having to work up a syllabus on 'justice.' This manual would be a worthwhile addition to any religion and/or social studies curriculum library." *Review for Religious*

"The resource volume is rich in ideas for a methodology of teaching Christian justice, and in identifying the problems. It is also very rich in the quality of the background readings provided. The participant's volume is a catchy workbook with many illustrations. It encourages the student (young or adult) to look at the problems as they are experienced by real live persons." *The Priest*

"Replete with background essays, tested group exercises, course outlines and annotated bibliography, this manual should give any teacher or seminar leader plenty of material to launch a thorough study program—and plenty of strongly stated positions for students to react to." *America*

ISBN 0-88344-154-3   *Resource Manual $7.95*
ISBN 0-88344-120-9   *Participant Workbook $3.95*

GUTIERREZ, Gustavo
A THEOLOGY OF LIBERATION

Selected by the reviewers of *Christian Century* as one of the twelve religious books published in the 1970s which "most deserve to survive."

"Rarely does one find such a happy fusion of gospel content and contemporary relevance." *The Lutheran Standard*

ISBN 0-88344-477-1   *Cloth $7.95*
ISBN 0-88344-478-X   *Paper $4.95*

HENNELLY, Alfred
THEOLOGIES IN CONFLICT
The Challenge of Juan Luis Segundo

"This is another, and a significant, addition to the growing literature on liberation theology. Hennelly's intent is to initiate a dialogue with Latin American theologians and thus foster an indigenous North American liberation theology. After two introductory chapters in which he situates and overviews this new movement, he focuses on Segundo's articulation of some central liberation themes: the relation between history and divine reality, the role of the church, theological method, spirituality, and the significance of Marxism. Throughout, he draws heavily on material not available in English. Hennelly does not write as a critic of but as a spokesperson for Segundo; yet his own convictions are evident when, at the end of each chapter, he extracts challenging questions for North Americans. He voices a growing awareness: the impossibility, the sinfulness, of carrying on theology detached from social-political realities. Definitely for most theology collections." *Library Journal*

"Father Hennelly provides an excellent introduction to Juan Segundo's thought and a helpful guide to the voluminous literature, presenting the theology not as 'systematic' but as 'open': methodological principles allowing for growth and development take precedence over systematic organization of concepts." *Paul Deats, Professor of Social Ethics, Boston University*

ISBN 0-88344-287-6   224pp. Paper $8.95

HERZOG, Frederick
JUSTICE CHURCH

The author, Professor of Systematic Theology at Duke Divinity School, continues the pioneering work he began with *Liberation Theology* (1972). *Justice Church* presents the *first* North American methodology of liberation theology while also critically analyzing what is and what should be the function of the Church in contemporary North America.

"Herzog refuses to do an easy or obvious theology, but insists on raising difficult questions which require theology to be done with some anguish. He has seen more clearly than most that we are in a crisis of categories, which must be reshaped in shattering ways." *Walter Brueggemann, Eden Theological Seminary*

"For us in Latin America, the question of how North Americans do theology is critically important. Besides its intrinsic value for the United States and Canada, this book should stimulate theological conversation across the North-South divide." *Jose Miguez Bonino, Dean of the Higher Institute of Theological Studies, Buenos Aires*

ISBN 0-88344-249-3   176pp. Paper $6.95

RAYAN, Samuel
THE HOLY SPIRIT
Heart of the Gospel and Christian Hope
"*The Holy Spirit* by Samuel Rayan, an important Indian theologian, gives a bold interpretation of the New Testament and of the central role of the Holy Spirit, a role which western Christianity has often neglected." *Cross Currents*

"This work has a freshness and vitality that is captivating and thought-provoking. It should be read slowly because Rayan speaks truth so simply and beautifully that I found my reading moving easily to reflection and prayer. It is a book not to be easily forgotten because it so well integrates the action of the Spirit with the call to do justice in the world. I hope it will have wide circulation since it can easily be a source for personal spiritual growth, a teaching resource for prayer communities and parish education groups, and a means of formation of Christian leaders." *Catholic Charismatic*

ISBN 0-88344-188-8   *Paper $5.95*

REILLY, Michael Collins, S.J.
SPIRITUALITY FOR MISSION
Historical, Theological, and Cultural Factors for a Present-Day Missionary Spirituality
"Reilly's thesis is that, since the nature of missionary work has changed in recent years and since the theology of mission is now in a state of development, the motivation and spirituality for the modern missionary must also change. *Spirituality for Mission* synthesizes much of the current discussion on mission work and the concerns related to missionary work. Much recent literature deals with missions, but the significance of this book is that it treats the person who is involved in missionary work. It sets forth the importance and value of the missionary vocation." *Theological Studies*
"The book is a rich one. Reilly's statements on evangelization and development, on the aims of mission, and other questions are clearer than many other statements published in recent years." *Philippine Studies*
ISBN 0-88344-464-X   *Paper $8.95*